William Birchley

A Selection of Hymns and Meditation

For every Day of the Week

William Birchley

A Selection of Hymns and Meditation
For every Day of the Week

ISBN/EAN: 9783337064525

Printed in Europe, USA, Canada, Australia, Japan

Cover: Foto ©Thomas Meinert / pixelio.de

More available books at **www.hansebooks.com**

A
SELECTION
OF
HYMNS
AND
MEDITATIONS.

ERRORS and OMISSIONS in the MEDITATIONS.

To Note II. Page 9, *add* St John chap. xiv. v. 6.
Page 13, *Line* 13, *for* too truly *read* how truly.
Page 20, *Line* 8, *for* fit *read* fit.
Page 28, *Line* 3, *for* fpakedft *read* fpakeft,
Place at the end of Line 2, *p.* 36, *a Semicolon inftead of the Period.*
Read Line 11 *of Page* 83 *without the Comma at* Life.
Page 89, *Note I. for* Ecclef. *read* Ecclus.

ERRORS in the ANNOTATIONS.

Page 110, *Line* 3, *for* Auften's *read* Auftin's.
Read Line 13 *of Page* 133 *with a Comma at* ut.
Page 148, *Line* 11, *for* originates from *read* originates in.
Page 150, *Line* 19, *for* cenforque *read* cenforque.
In the Note to Amaranth, Page 161, *place a Colon at* HARTE:
  and read He was the Tutor.

too highly figurative *Expreſſions.* *The Reading of an old Manuſcript Selection (from the unreformed Devotions, its Date the Reign of Charles II.) is ſometimes preferred to that of Dr Hicks' Editions ; for the Force of Sentiments is often weakened by modernizing the Language. Thoſe Sentences are reduced wherein a Thought ſeemed too much extended. The Hymns that are ſelected are, in general, untouched : They are better ſeen in their native* Simplicity. *The Scriptures are referred to, where a Confirmation or Illuſtration ſeemed neceſſary ; and ſuch References are ſet before the Reader in every Page as they occur.*

Extracts, as well from Authors that are generally known, as from thoſe moral and religious Writings which are now read only by a few, are added, with occaſional Remarks, in an Appendix. 'Tis pleaſing to obſerve the various Modes of expreſſing the ſame Thoughts, (though it has ſometimes happened that Men have not only thought, but expreſſed their Sentiments alike †) and to trace to its Source the Improvements of a more fertile Imagination upon a bare Idea ſuggeſted by a former writer, which a ſucceeding one, having enriched and extended

---

* This Term may be deemed ill applied to the Hymn for Thurſday Morning, which is very *figurative :* But in general the Hymns are plain and ſimple.

† The Reader will meet with ſeveral Inſtances of an exact Similarity both in the Sentiments and Expreſſions of Authors, who were unacquainted with the Writings of each other, in Wharton's excellent " Eſſay on the Writings and Genius of Pope."——See Vol. i. p. 91, 92, 93.

into many finer Branches, claims as his Right, and en-
grafts upon his own Work.

I have presumed to contrast the Sentiments of a few
Heathen Writers, as proofs in point of the infinite advantages which result from Revelation; though sensible that
in a Work of this kind such Quotations are exceptionable:
But, lest the attention of the devout Reader should be di-
verted from the main Subject by placing them at the foot
of each Page, all the Extracts and Annotations are sub-
joined in an Appendix.

Vain would be the Expectation, and even the Wish,
that every one who takes up this Book may reap from it
the Pleasure and Instruction which its Editor received:
For it is impossible to wipe off the Scales of Prejudice
from every Eye, and some read but to find fault. He
may, however, be permitted to indulge an Hope, that they
who read it with a desire to receive Pleasure and Improvement, will not be disappointed in their Expectations.
Encouraged by this Hope, he ventures to restore to Light
what has long lien in anmerited Obscurity; (D) and if
by his means one pious Thought be excited in a careless
Heart, the Design of this Publication will, in some
measure, be attained, and his Labours blessed.

H. COTES.

Bedlington, April 29, 1791.

The PREFACE.

THE following Selection is made from a Book * that was many years ago reformed, in part, from the Errors of the Church of Rome, and has since been given to the world in various Editions by several hands. Two Editions of it were published in the form of " Offices for " every day in the week, with additional Hymns, Pray- " ers, &c." by Dr George Hicks, Dean of Worcester, whose Character for Probity, Piety, and Learning is well known.

The Pleasure and Instruction which I received from a Book that is now scarcely known, and, where it is known, for obvious reasons seldom read, induce me to offer a Selection of its Hymns and Meditations (Note A) to the Protestant Christian Reader ; that he whose mind is at-tuned to holy things, who has a relish for those pure plea-sures that spring from the Love of God, may likewise en-joy the beauties of these Compositions, which, whilst they warm, correct the heart.

I do not think myself bound to answer every objection that may be cast on a Publication so ill adapted to the Taste of the Times.— It bears so little of the Rust of Anti-quity, as to preclude all reliance on that Recommendation ; for however the Antique, and, in some cases, its slightest Vestige, be a sure way to public favour, with regard to Re-

* Austin's Devotions, lately published in its original state for the use of Papists.

ligion and Religious Writings it is the reverfe.   But the
Neceffity *enforceth the* Obligation *on every fincere Chrif-*
tian to contribute his beft, though it be a Mite, to correct
the falfe Tafte of the Age; and, whilft he endeavours to
turn it from the purfuit of vanity, to quicken its Relifh
for the true, fubftantial Pleafures of Religion.

   The Meditations — to pafs by the Plan *of the Book*
whence they are felected — bear a near refemblance, as
to their Rhythm, (B) *to our Tranflation of the Book of*
Pfalms, *from which the Author* † *has taken many Ima-*
ges and Expreffions.   I know not whether to term them
Compofitions of Profe or Verfe; they are not indeed re-
gularly *metrical, and the returning line and verficle too*
frequently anfwer to the meafure of the preceding for
mere profe : *They may be called —* Numerous Profe
Compofitions.   *But, however, the frequent and appo-*
fite metaphorical Allufions with which they are embellifh-
ed, *render them truly poetical.* (C)   *The Reading is often*
varied left the ear fhould be fatigued by the reiterating
of the fame meafure.   A Motto, taken from Scripture,
indicative of the Subject that follows, is prefixed to each
Meditation, inftead of the Antiphone *with which, in*
the Original, the Pfalms *are introduced and clofed.*
Such Sentences as but *favoured of the* Roman Opinions
are either altered or entirely omitted.   I have likewife
ventured to alter fome, perhaps too warm, *and others*

---

   † For Particulars relative to his Life and Character, the Reader is
referred to the Preface to the new Edition of Auftin's Devotions,
printed at Edinburgh, 1789.

SUNDAY MORNING.

H y m n I.

BEHOLD, I come, O! Lord, to Thee,
   And bow before thy Throne;
I come to offer on my Knee
My Vows to Thee alone!

Whate'er we have, whate'er we are,
   Thy Bounty freely gave;
Thou doſt us here in Mercy ſpare,
And wilt hereafter ſave.

But, O! can all our Store afford
   No better Gifts to Thee?
Thus I confeſs thy Riches, Lord!
And thus my Poverty.

'Tis not my Tongue or Knee can pay
   The mighty Debt I owe;
Far more I would, than I can ſay,
Far lower would I bow.

Come then, my Soul, bring all thy Pow'rs,
   And grieve thou haſt no more;
Bring every Day thy choiceſt Hours,
And thy great God adore.

A

But, above all, prepare thy Heart,
On this his own bleſt Day,
In the ſweet Taſk to bear its Part,
And ſing, and love, and pray.

SUNDAY MORNING.

Meditation I.

" *This is the Day our Lord hath made, let us rejoice and*
be glad in it."   Pſal. cxviii. 24.

WELCOME, bleſt Day! whereon the Sun of
         Righteouſneſs aroſe,
and chaſed away the Clouds of Fear!
   Welcome, thou Birth-day of Man's Hopes;
a Day of Joy and Refreſhment; a Day of Holineſs and
         Devotion!
   Welcome to this dark World! may every Mind
be enlightened by thy Beams, and every frozen Heart
         diſſolve and ſing,
   " This is the Day our Lord hath made,
" let us rejoice and be glad therein."
   This is the Day He hath ſanctified to himſelf,
and called by his own moſt holy Name;

That in it we may meet to adore his Greatnefs,
and thankfully dwell upon the Multitude of his Mercies;
.That we may vifit his holy Temple,
and humbly prefent ourfelves at his Altar ;
 Where the Sacrifice of the Lamb is duly fhewn,
the Memory of a Saviour's Love continually renew'd ;
 Where the contrite Spirit pours forth its Vows,
and the faithful Penitent is affur'd of Pardon.
 Worthy art Thou, O Lord! of all my Time,
as Thou art worthy of all my Praife :
 Every Moment of my Life is bound to blefs Thee,
fince every Moment fubfifts by thy Goodnefs :
 Shall I employ the whole Week on myfelf,
and not offer in Gratitude one Day to Thee ?
 To Thee—who beftow'ft on me all I have,
and wilt give me hereafter more than I can hope ?
 O gracious Lord! whofe Mercy accepts
fuch flender Payments as Man's Poverty affords; *
 Whofe Bounty grants fo liberally to him,
and retains fo fmall a portion to Thyfelf ;
 Make me faithfully to obferve my Duty,
and render fo exactly the Tribute I owe to Thee;
 That, paffing ftill *thy* Days to thy Honour,
I may end *my own* in thy Favour !

* Note I.

A 2

MEDITATION II.

" *But unto you that fear my Name, fhall the Sun of Righteoufnefs arife with Healing in his Wings.*" Mal. iv. 2.

WHEN the Harveft Sun provides a Cloud,
    and feems to reft his wearied Beams,
'Tis not to fave the Journey of his Light,
but to fpare the Reaper's Head.
Much lefs feek'ft Thou, O Lord! who mad'ft the Sun
the Shadow of thy Glory, and infpir'ft all Creatures to
    reprefent thy Bounty;
Much lefs feek'ft Thou, by the Referve of a Day,
to procure thine own Repofe:
Nor is it to increafe thine own Eternity,
that thus Thou tak'ft a Portion of our Time.
Thy Goodnefs friendlily bears the Name,
but intends for us all the Profit of the Day;
That the wearied Hands may be reliev'd by Reft,
and enabled to lift themfelves up to Thee;
That the ignorant Minds may be taught thy Truths,
and learn the Way to Happinefs;
That the guilty Confcience may bewail its Crimes,
and be footh'd with the Hopes of Pardon and Peace;
That the contrite Souls may approach thy Table,
and ftrengthen their Faith in Thee their Saviour;

That all may fpeak to Thee by Prayer, (1)
and hear thy Voice by the Mouth of thy Minifters.

O bleffed Lord! how admirably does thy Wifdom
contrive
to bring us to Thyfelf!

Thou quick'neft our Affections by our mutual Devotions,

Thou ftrength'neft our Faith, and improv'ft our Charity, by thy public Affemblies;

While we all meet together for the fame blefs'd End,
and by alternate Reflections increafe our Fervours.

Happy they! whom thy Providence has favour'd
with all thefe Bleffings!

But to whom Thou art pleafed to deny fuch Mercies,
refufe not to extend thy Grace!

Be Thou but prefent, gracious God!
and fill them with thy Love;

No ftronger Motives will they need to draw them,
no *other* (2) Temple to addrefs their Prayers;

Since every Place where Thou art not, is unholy;
and where Thou art, is Joy and Peace.

(1) *Pfalm* lxv. 2.—O Thou that hearcft Prayer, unto Thee fhall all
Flefh come!

(2) 1 *Cor.* iii. 16.—Know ye not that'ye are the Temple of God,
and that the Spirit of God dwelleth in you?

MEDITATION III.

" How dear are thy Counfels unto me, O God — O how great is the Sum of them!" Pfal. cxxxix. 17.

*THE Lord of Life is rifen, and hath cloathed
  himfelf with immortal Glory !

He made the Angels Meffengers (3) of his Victory,

and Himfelf vouchfafed to bring the joyful Tidings. (4)

How many Ways, O Lord ! did thy Wifdom invent
  to convince thy Followers,

and to fettle in their Hearts a firm Ground of Hope !

Thou appearedft to the Women (5) on their Return
  from the Sepulchre,

and openedft their Eyes to know and adore Thee.

Thou didft o'ertake in the Way (6) the two that dif-
  courfed of Thee,

and madeft their Hearts to (7) acknowledge thy Prefence.

Thou fhewedft thyfelf on the Shore, (8)

to thy weary Difciples labouring at Sea ;

Labouring all Night, alas ! in vain,

without the Bleffing of their beloved Mafter :

---

* Note II.

(3) St Mark xvi. 6.—St Luke xxiv. 6.   (4) St John xx. 17, 19.
(5) St Mark xvi. 12.   (6) St Luke xxiv. 13.
(7) St Luke xxiv. 32.   (8) St John xxi. 4.

Thou revealedft thyfelf to them,
in the kind, known (9) Token of a beneficial Miracle.
Thro' the Doors, when fhut, (1) thou fwiftly paffedft,
to carry Peace to thy comfortlefs Difciples.
How didft Thou condefcend to eat (2) before them,
and invite them to touch thy then, impaffible, Body!
How didft Thou provoke the incredulous Thomas,
(3) to thruft his Hand into thy wounded Side!
Actions unfuitable to thy glorified State,
but neceffary to our flow Belief!
When at length thy Tafk was done,
and thy parting Hour from this Earth approach'd;
Thou tenderly gatheredft (4) thy Children about
    Thee,
and in their full Sight afcendedft to Heav'n:
Leaving thy deareft Bleffing on their Heads,
and promifing them a Comforter to fupply thine Ab-
    fence.
" O how wonderful are thy Counfels, O Lord!
How great is the Sum of them!"
What tho' I mourn and be afflicted here,
and figh under the Miferies of this World for a Time;
I truft that my Tears fhall be turned into Joy;
a Joy which no one fhall take from me!

---

(9) St Luke v. 4.—Not the *firft* Miracle of this Kind.
(1) St John xx. 19.   (2) St John xxi. 13.   (3) St John xx. 27.
(4) St Luke xxiv. 50.

I know that my Redeemer liveth, (5)
who will appear at the laſt Great Day :
  I ſhall ſee Him in whom I have ſo long believed,
I ſhall find Him whom I have ſo often ſought :
  I ſhall poſſeſs Him whom my Soul has loved,*
and be united to Him for ever who is the only End of
    my Being.

MEDITATION IV.

" *He was received into Heaven, and fat on the Right-Hand of God.*" St Mark xvi. 19.

AWAKE, O my Soul! behold the Glory
    of thy crucified Saviour !
  He, who died and was laid in the Grave,
to prove himſelf Man ;
  Is riſen and aſcended into Heaven,
to prove himſelf GOD.
  He is riſen — and hath made the Light his Garment,
and the Clouds the Chariot of his Triumph :
  The Gates of Heav'n obey'd their Lord,
and the everlaſting Doors opened to the King of
    Glory. (6)

(5) Job xix. 25.   (6) Pſalm xxiv. 7.
* Note III.

Whom have I in Heaven, O Lord! but Thee;
who returnedft thither to prepare (1) a Place for thy
     Followers:
Whom have I on Earth but Thee, my Hope,
to lead me at laft whither Thou art gone before?
O Saviour! my Strength, my Joy,
and the immortal Life of my Soul!
Draw (2) me from the World, and from myfelf,
that I be not entangled with earthly Defires!
Draw me, and I will follow Thee to thy Throne of
     Blifs,
and rejoice with Thee for ever in thy Kingdom.

---

(1) St John xiv. 2.
(2) No Man cometh unto the Father but by me.

SUNDAY EVENING.

H y m n   II.

O SAVIOUR! when, when will it be
That I no more fhall break with Thee!
When will this War of Paffions ceafe,
And let my Soul enjoy thy Peace! ?

Here, I repent, and fin again; *
Now I revive, and now am flain:
Slain with the fame unhappy Dart,
Which, ah! fo often wounds my Heart.

When, gracious Lord, when fhall I be
A Garden feal'd to all but Thee;
No more expos'd, no more undone,
But live and grow to Thee alone!

'Tis not, alas! on this low Earth
That fuch pure Flow'rs can find a Birth:
They only fpring above the Skies,
Where none can live till here he dies.

* Note IV.

Then let me die, that I may go
And dwell where thofe bright Lillies grow;
Where thofe bleft Plants of Glory rife,
And make a fafer Paradife!

MEDITATION V.

—"*A Shadow of good Things to come.*" Heb. x. 1.

LET them, O Lord! feek other Delights,
  who expect no Rewards from Thee.
  As for me, my Joy on Earth fhall be,
to meditate the Happinefs of Hereafter:
  All the few Years I live fhall lay themfelves out
to purchafe that one eternal Day;
  That Day, whofe Brightnefs knows no Night, *
nor fears the leaft Eclipfe;
  Whofe chearful Brow no Cloud o'ercafts,
nor Storm molefts the Paffage of its Rays;
  But ever fhines ferene,
and fills with its Splendor the Heaven of Heav'ns.
  It needs not the fading Luftre of our Sun,
nor the borrow'd Silver of the Moon:

* Note V.

The Sun that rifeth there (1) is the Lamb,
and the Light that fhines the Glory of God.

O! how beauteous things are written of Thee,
Thou City of the King of Heaven!

Thy Manfions are built of choiceft Jewels,
and the Pavement of thy Streets is Gold: (2)

Down in the midft runs a chryftal River, (3)
perpetually flowing from the Throne of God;

Whofe Banks are crown'd with the Tree of Life,
which healeth all Wounds and giveth Immortality. †

Thus is the New Jerufalem adorn'd.
O! glorious City! how happy are thine Inhabitants!

Every Head wears a Crown, and every Hand
a Palm of Victory: (4)

Every Eye o'erflows with Joy,
and ev'ry Tongue with Pfalms of Praife.

Behold! O my Soul! the Inheritance we feek;
the Joys, to which we are called!

Away, then, ye worldly Defires, be banifh'd
from molefting my Peace!

Defcend Thou bleft Heaven into my Heart!
or --- take up my Heart to Thee!

Thy Joys are too great to enter into me;
O make me fit to enter into them!

---

(1) Rev. xxi. 23.   (2) Rev. xxi. 18.   (3) Rev. xxii. 1, 2.
(4) Rev. vii. 9.
† Note VI.

Make me ftill meditate on my Country above,
there to eftablifh an eternal Home,

Where I fhall dwell in the View cf my God,
and be for ever filled with the Glory of his Prefence.

M E D I T A T I O N   VI.

" *As the Heavens are higher than the Earth, fo are my Ways higher than your Ways, and my Thoughts than your Thoughts, faith the Lord.*"   Ifaiah lv. 9.

BLESS'D be thy Wifdom, O Lord!
  that fo mercifully ftoops to our low Conceits!
  Under thefe Veils thou hid'ft thy glorious Myfteries,
too high and fpiritual for Flefh and Blood :
  Thou hid'ft, or rather fo revealeft, thy fublime
        Rewards,
as to take us with the Things we moft admire.
  Sceptres and Crowns, Thou know'ft,
are apt to win the Hearts of us thy Children ; *
  Children, alas! too truly in ufeful Knowledge —
O! that we were fo in Love and Duty !

* Note VII.

What is a Drop of Water to the boundlefs Ocean,
or a Grain of Duft to this vaft Globe?

Such, and infinitely lefs, are the richeft Kingdoms
on Earth,
to the meaneft Degree in Heav'n.

When Thou haft fed us a while with Milk,
Thou invit'ft our Appetite to ftronger Meat:　　.

Thou tell'ft us of a Life of Happinefs,
in the bleft Society of Saints and Angels,

Thou tell'ft us of ftill higher Joys ——
hearken, O my Soul! with humble Reverence ——

Himfelf Th' ETERNAL will unveil,
and openly fhew us that Great Secret. *

What is it, Lord! to fee thy Face,
but to know Thee as Thou art in thy Self-exifting
Effence?

To know the Power of the everlafting Father,
the Love and Wifdom of the increated Son:

To know the Goodnefs of the Holy Ghoft,
and to dwell in the Glories of the undivided Trinity.

This, O my Soul! is the height of Happinefs,
this the Perfection † of our Nature:

This, this alone, the aim of our being,
the hope and end of all our labours.

* Note VIII.　　　　† Note IX.

When we are come to this, we reſt,
and our ſatisfied deſires reach no farther ;
   But in one act of Joy are *eternally* fix'd ——
for that one act ſprings freſh for ever. ‡

══════════

MEDITATION   VII.

" *All the Days of my appointed Time will I wait 'till
my Change come.*" Job xiv. 14.

ARISE! my Soul! to thee theſe joys belong,
   lift up thyſelf on high!
Hail, happy Paradiſe of pure Delights!
Hail, bleſt Society of Saints and Angels!
   Hail, ye, who in your Hymns remember them
that dwell in this Vale of Miſery!
   I hope one Day to join you, and to know and praiſe
the all-producing Cauſe.
   When, without loſing what I am,
I ſhall become even what He is.
   Neither hath the Eye ſeen, Ear heard, (1)
nor can the Heart of Man conceive the joys of Heav'n.

---

‡ Note X.   (1) 1 Cor. ii. 9.

There I fhall reft from Sin and Sorrow,
no longer to be troubled with myfelf or others.

O Lord! the eternal Source of all thefe Joys,
and infinitely more, and infinitely greater;

" As the Hart panteth after the Water-brooks," (2)
fo let my Soul thirft after Thee:

For my Sins let me daily figh and mourn,
in Faith look up to Thee, and fay,

" When fhall I reft at the Fountain-head,
" and drink of the Streams which flow for ever from
        thy Throne?!

" O that the Days of my Banifhment were ended,*
" how is the Time of my Pilgrimage prolong'd!

" Why am I ftill detain'd in this Valley of Tears,
" ftill wand'ring up and down in this Wildernefs of
        " Dangers!?

" Come, my Deliverer, and here begin to dwell in
    " my Heart,

" and fit me for the Life I hope to lead hereafter!

" Come, Lord! and prepare my Soul for Heav'n,
" and then, when Thou pleafeft, take it to thyfelf!"

(2) Pfalm xlii. 1.   * Note XI.

MEDITATION   VIII.

" Blessed are the Poor in Spirit, for theirs is the King-
dom of Heaven." St Matt. v. 3.

GIVE me, O Lord! the Innocence of a Dove,
  and fill my Soul with thy mild Spirit,
Then shall I not need its Wings,*
for the Kingdom of Heaven (1) will dwell in my Heart.
  On the Proud Thou lookest afar off,
but inclin'st thine Ear to the humble and meek;
  Who never intermeddle with the actions of others,
unless where Charity engageth them.
  How sweetly do they sleep,
who retire to rest with a quiet Conscience!
, Who after a day of faithful Industry,
in a Course of just and pious living,
  Lay down their wearied Heads in Peace,
and safely rest in the Bosom of Providence.
  This too, my Soul, should be thy Care,
to note, and censure, and correct thyself: †

---

* Note XII.   † Note X.II.
(1) Isa. lvii. 15.—And St Luke xvii. 21.

C

Let, then, the worldly follow their ways;
for what are their ways to thee,
who fhalt not anfwer for others if thou partake not
    in their fins. (2)
Thy Pity may grieve, and thy Charity endeavour,
but if they will not hear, follow thou thy God.
Follow the Footfteps of thy Saviour,
who alone is " the Way, the Truth, and the Life : " (3)
Follow his Holinefs in what He did,
his Patience in what He fuffered :
Follow thy (4) faithful Lord to the End,
and thou art fure in the End to poffefs Him for ever.

MEDITATION   IX.

" *Whether we live or die, we are the Lord's.*"   Rom. xiv. 8,

MEEKNESS is the Heav'n of this Life,
    will qualify my Miferies, and make my Time
    pafs gently away :
But to be fully happy I muft wait till hereafter,
till thy Mercy, O God, lead me to mine End ;
That glorious End, for which Mankind was made,
and all things vifible, to ferve us on our way.

(1) 1 Tim. v. 22.   (3) St John xiv. 6.
(4) Heb. x. 23.—" He is faithful who promifed,"

'Twas not to fport our Time in Pleafures,
that Thou didft place us here :
But to do good to ourfelves and others,
and glorify Thee fh improving thy Creatures :
To increafe every Day our Defire
of beholding Thee as Thou art, in thine own bright *Self.*
—— May my Affections, *therefore*, delight in Thee,
above all the vain Employments of this World !
Above all Praife and empty Honour, .
above all Beauty and fading Pleafure !
May I * deny (5) myfelf to follow Thee,
and fill my Memory with the Wonders of thy Love:
    That infinite Love, which when my Thoughts con-
        fider,
not as it deferves, but as they're able,
The Goods and Ills of this Life lofe their Name, .
and yield not either Relifh or Diftafte.
Let me then love Thee alone, my Saviour,
† becaufe (6) Thou alone deferveft all my Heart.
    " Glory be to the Father, and to the Son, and to
        " the Holy Ghoft ——
" as it was in the beginning, is now, and ever fhall be
    " World without end." *Amen !*

---

* Note XIV.   † Note XV.
(5) St Matt. xvi. 24.
(6) We love God becaufe he firft loved us.—1 John iv. 19.

MONDAY MORNING.

H y m n   III.

WAKE now, my Soul, and humbly hear
   What thy mild Lord commands!
Each Word of his will charm thine Ear,
Each Word will guide thine Hands.

Hark! how his kind and tender Care
Complies with our weak Minds;
Whate'er our State and Tempers are,
Still some fit Work he finds.

They that are merry, let them sing,
And let the sad Hearts pray;
Let those still ply their chearful Wing,
And these their sober Day.

So mounts the early warbling Lark
Still upwards to the Skies;
So sits the Turtle in the Dark
Amidst her plaintive Cries.

And yet the Lark and yet the Dove
Both fing, tho' diff'rent Parts;
And fo fhould we, howe'er we move,
With light or heavy Hearts.

Or rather we fhould, each, affay
And our crofs notes unite;
Both Grief and Joy fhould fing and pray,
Since both fuch Hopes invite.

Hopes that all prefent Sorrow heal,
All prefent Joy tranfcend;
Hopes to poffefs, and tafte, and feel
Delights that never end.

MEDITATION X.

" Thou art about my Bed and about my Path, and
fpieft out all my Ways." Pfalm cxxxix. 2.

HAPPY are they, who every where
adore their Maker!
   Who live on Earth as in the Sight of the
King of Heaven, and can always fay in their Hearts,
" Our God is here!"

Tho' his Throne of State be eſtabliſh'd above,
and the Splendors of his Glory ſhine only on the Bleſſed,
   Yet, his unlimited Eye looks down on this lower
      World,
and beholds all the Ways of the Children of Adam. *
   When I go out, He marks my Steps; and when I
      retire,
my cloſet excludes him not. (1)
   If I deceive my Neighbour, He ſpies the Fraud,
and hears the leaſt Whiſper of a ſlandering Tongue.
   If in ſecret I oppreſs the Poor; or by Alms
relieve their Wants;
   If in my Heart I murmur at the Rich,
or live contented with my little Portion:
   Whate'er I do, He perfectly ſees me; where'er I am,
my God is with me.
   What canſt Thou find, O Lord, that here deſerves
      thy Sight,
amidſt the Trifles of our empty World;
   What canſt Thou find, alas! that ſhould not fear
      thy Sight,
amidſt the Follies of our vicious Lives?!
   Thou graciouſly ſtandeſt by to ſee us work,
that thine awful Eye may quicken our Diligence;
   Thou art ſtill at hand to relieve our Wants,
that ſo friendly a nearneſs may increaſe our Confidence;

* Note XVI.   (1) Pſalm cxxxix. 3.

Thou appeareſt ſtill ready to puniſh our Sins,
that the Shake of thy Rod may prevent our Miſeries.

Surely thy Favours muſt needs engage us,
ſince even thy Threat'nings have ſo much Mercy:

Surely we muſt be worſe than blind,
if to thy very Face we dare be wicked.

—— Henceforth, O gracious Lord! as a Child
freely plays in the Preſence of an indulgent Father;

So make me ſtill, with humble Boldneſs,
rejoice before Thee, my merciful Creator.

O temper thus my Love with Reverence,
and thus allay my Fear with Hope! †

MEDITATION XI.

" Aſk, and ye ſhall have; ſeek, and ye ſhall find; knock, and it ſhall be opened unto you." St Matt. vii. 7.

MY God! ſince Thou art never abſent from me,
let me be always preſent with Thee:

Every where let me ſeek Thee,* every where
let me delight to find Thee.

† Note XVII.   * Note XVIII.

Thou willingly inclineſt thine Ear
to the Prayers that come from a fervent Heart;
  If Thou ſometimes defer to grant my Requeſts, †
'tis only in Charity to make me repeat them:

  That I may more ſenſibly feel my own Poverty,
and be more ſtrongly convinced of my Dependance on
        Thee:

  That I may practiſe my Hope while I long expect,
and increaſe my Gratitude when I at laſt receive:

  That I may learn this happy Skill
of working in my Soul the Virtues I deſire;
  By often renewing thoſe very Deſires
till theirſelves become the Graces I ſeek. ‡

  But—O improvident Man!—How unwilling to pray
are moſt of us always, and the beſt of us ſometimes!

  As for me, O Lord! often when I ſpeak to Thee
I do not ſo much as hear myſelf. §

  Often I purſue impertinent Objects,
and my careleſs Thoughts contradict my Words.

  Yet ſtill I have new Tranſgreſſions to confeſs,
and ſhall never want Infirmities to lament.

  But, O Thou bleſſed End of my Labours,
and only Center of my Wiſhes,
  Reclaim my wand'ring Fancy,
and fix it on thy Service!

---

† Note XIX.   ‡ Note XX.   § Note XXI.

Night and Day let me call on Thee,
nor ceafe to knock till the Door be opened.

Let no Delay difcourage, nor even Refufal
deftroy my Confidence;

But on this firm Foundation let me ftay,
" What's truly needful thy Goodnefs will grant,
" the reft my Obedience fubmits to thy Pleafure."

MEDITATION XII.

" *Ye afk and receive not, becaufe ye afk amifs.*"

St James iv. 3.

DELIVER me, O Lord! from afking of Thee,
what I cannot receive without danger to myfelf!
Deliver me from fo prefuming on thy Bounty,
as to neglect my own Duty!

Still to my Devotion let me join Endeavours,
and fo make Earth comply with Heaven.

If I implore Thee to relieve my Neceffities,
let me faithfully labour with my Hands;

And not expect a Bleffing from the Clouds
on the idle Follies of an undifciplin'd Life.

D

When I beg Grace for Victory o'er my Paffions,
let me conftantly ftrive to refift their Affaults :

Let me wifely forefee my particular (1) Danger,
and ufe a fit Weapon againft every Sin.

To obtain the Gift of Chaftity I muft mortify Senfe,
and flee from the flighteft Temptation.

Fór in vain I approach thy holy Altar,
if my Life prepare not the way for my Offerings. *

Thou fhutteft thine Ears to my loudeft Prayers,
if I open not mine to the Voice of the Poor. .

Thou denieft to pardon my Trefpaffes againft Thee,
if I have not already forgiven mine offending Brother.

O the extreme Benignity of our God,
who treats with his Creatures upon equal Terms !

Who deals no otherwife with us miferable wretches
than we ourfelves *commerce* † with each other !

He promifes to give us the Meafure we give our
     Neighbours,
and performs more than he promifes ;

(2) " Preffed down, and fhaken together, and run-
     " ning over,

" into the Bofoms of them that love him."

Such, O my God ! is the Bounty of thy Goodnefs,
and fuch the Patience of thy generous Hand :

Thou holdeft thy Bleffings hov'ring o'er our Heads,
ftill watching the Time we are fit to receive them :

(1) Heb. xii. 1.   * Note XXII.   † Note XXIII.   (2) St Luke vi. 38.

And even that Temper which difpofeth us for thy
  Bleffings,
entirely depends upon thy Favour;
 Every Condition Thou requireft on our Part,
being nothing elfe than thine own free Gift.
 Thy Mercy alone is the Fountain of all our Bleffings,
and in what Channel foever they flow to us, *
they fpring from Thee.

<hr />

M E D I T A T I O N   XIII.

 " *Praife the Lord, O my Soul, and all that is within
me praife his holy Name.*" Pfal. ciii. 1.

TOO glorious art Thou, O Lord! in thyfelf,
 and thy direct Rays fhine too bright for our Eyes;
The Voice of Angels is too low to reach thy Worth,
and their higheft Strains fall infinitely fhort of Thee;
 How dare † we then attempt thy Praifes,
how dare our fin-polluted lips pronounce thy Name!
 Yet we may venture to praife Thee in thy Works,
and contemplate Thee reflected from thy Creatures;

  * Note XXIV,   † Note XXV,

Every Element is filled with thy Wifdom,
and all the World with thy liberal Miracles.

Thou fpakedft, and they were made;
Thou commandeft, and they are preferved:

Thou governeft their Motions in perfect Order,
and diftributeft to each its proper Office;

Contriving the whole into one vaft Machine,
a fpacious THEATRE OF THY GREATNESS.

O glorious Architect of univerfal Nature,
who difpofeft all things in number, weight, and meafure;

How doth thy Wifdom engage us to adore,
and thy Goodnefs oblige (3) us to love Thee!

Nor for themfelves alone, O gracious God!
did thy Hand produce the happy Spirits;

But to receive in Charge (4) thy little Flock,
and fafe conduct it to the Folds of Blifs.

Not for itfelf at all
was this vifible Creation form'd;

But to fuftain our Lives in the Way,
and carry us on to our eternal Home.

——O may I praife Thee, Lord! for all thy Gifts,
but above all ftill value the Giver!

May every Bleffing be a Motive of Gratitude,
and every Creature a ftep of approach towards Thee!

So fhall I faithfully obferve their End,
and happily arrive at mine;

(3) 2 Cor. v. 14.   (4) Heb. i. 14.

Using them only as appointed Means
to prepare me for the Life of Heaven.

But have I well confidered the End of my own Being,
and faithfully complied with thy Purpofe to fave me?

No —— I frequently neglect thy Rules,
and my Actions are the Effects of Humour or Chance.

But — Pardon, O Lord! my paft Ingratitude,
and mercifully direct my Time to come:

Make my Senfes fubject to Reafon,
and my Reafon obedient to thy Will.

This is the Praife, this the Honor
Thou requireft of Man ;

That by obferving the Orders Thou appointeft him
here,
in this lower region of motion and change,

He may grow up to be happy hereafter,
in a State of Permanency and eternal Reft.

MONDAY EVENING,

H y m n   IV.

NOW, my Soul, the Day is done
    Which in the Morn was thine;
Now its Glaſs no more doth run,
Its Sun no longer ſhine.

True — alas ! the Day is gone ;
O ! were it only ſo !
Is't not loſt as well as done ?
Caſt up your 'counts and know,

Are we ſo much nearer Heav'n,
As to the Grave we bow ?
Has our Sorrow made all even,
And clear'd the Debts we owe ?

From what Vice have we refrain'd,
To break the Courſe of Sin ?
What new Virtue have we gain'd,
To make us rich within ?

Time is well beftow'd on thofe
Who well their Time beftow;
Whofe main Concern ftill forward goes,
Whofe Hopes ftill riper grow.

Who, whene'er the Clocks proclaim
" Another Hour is paft,"
Have an Art to fet their Aim,
And Thoughts upon their laft ——

That, their laft and happieft Hour,
Which brings them to their Home;
Where they fing and praife the Pow'r,
That made them thither come.

O my God of Life and Death,
My ever-living King,
Since Thou giv'ft to all their Breath,
May all thy Glory fing!

MEDITATION XIV.

" To know Thee is perfect Righteousness; yea, to know thy Power is the Root of Immortality." Wisd. xv. 3.

LET me consider, O God, let me thankfully remember,
what Thou art to Man.

Thou art the Great Beginning of our nature,
the Glorious End of all our actions:

Thou art the overflowing Source whence we spring,
and the immense Ocean into which we tend: *

The free Bestower of all we possess,
and faithful Promiser of future Blessings:

The merciful Scourger of our Sins,
and bounteous Rewarder of our Obedience:

The safe Conductor of our Pilgrimage,
and the Eternal Rest of wearied Souls.

Such Words our Narrowness is constrained to use,
when we endeavour to express thy Bounties:

Wider a little can our Thoughts extend,
yet infinitely less than the least of thy Mercies.

—— Tell me thyself, O Thou mild Instructor
of the Ignorant, what Thou art to me!

Say to my Soul " I am thy Salvation," (1)
but say it so that I may feel it.

* Note XXVI.   (1) Psalm xxxv. 3.

Meditation XV.

" What is Man, that Thou art mindful of him — and the Son of Man, that Thou so regardest him ? "   Psal. viii. 4.

" The thoughts of" man's " heart only evil."   Gen. vi. 5.

LET me now confider, O God! let me humbly remember,
what Man is to Thee.

We, who are nothing in ourfelves,
what can we be to thy Immenfity!

Thou — who art all things in thine own rich Fulnefs;
—— what canft Thou receive from our Poverty!

This only we are to Thee, O great Creator!
the unthankful Objects of thy Bounty :

. This only we are to Thee, O dear Redeemer!
the unworthy Caufe of thy Sufferings.

Guilty we committed the Crime, and Thou
with thine Innocency fuftainedft the Punifhment.

We went aftray from the Path of Life,
and thy Mercy came to feek, and to bring us home
to the Difcipline of thy Love.

E

Thou knoweſt the Danger of our wilful Nature;
and therefore ſtriv'ſt, by greateſt Fears and greateſt
      Hopes,
   And all the wiſeſt Arts of Love,
to draw us to Thyſelf, and endow us with thy Kingdom.
   Unhappy we! whoſe Frowardneſs requires ſo ſtrange
      Proceedings
to force upon us our own Salvation!
   Happy we! whoſe wants have met with ſo kind a
      Hand,
that needed but our Emptineſs to engage him to fill it!
   Happy yet more, ſince our Lord, who ſo favours us
      now,
will crown us at the laſt with his own Rewards!

M E D I T A T I O N   XVI.

" *The Day is thine, and the Night is thine; Thou
haſt prepared the Light and the Sun.*" Pſal. lxxiv. 17.

IN every thing, O God! I ſee thy Hand,
   in every Event thy gracious Providence.
   Thou wiſely governeſt the Houſe Thou haſt built,
and preventeſt with thy Mercies all our Wants:

Thou calleſt us forth in the Morning,
and ſheddeſt light by the Beams of thy Sun;
　That every one may labour in his Station,
and fill the Place appointed for him in the World.
　Thou provideſt a Reſt for the Evening,
and favoureſt our Sleep with Darkneſs;
　To refreſh our Bodies in the Shade of Night,
and reſtore the Waſte of our decaying Spirits.
　Thus hath thy Wiſdom mix'd our Life,
and beauteouſly interwoven it of Reſt and Work;
　Whoſe mutual Changes ſweeten each other,
and both prepare us for our greateſt Duty;
　Of finiſhing here the Work of our Salvation,
to reſt hereafter in thy holy Peace.

MEDITATION XVII.

" *My Times are in thy Hand.*" Pſal. xxxi. 15.

THY Bounty yields all other Things, O Lord!
　with a large and open Hand——
Our Fields at once are covered with Corn,
and Thou ſendeſt whole Show'rs of other Bleſſings;
　Only our Time Thou diſtill'ſt by Drops,
and never giveſt us two moments at once;

But takeſt away one when Thou lendeſt another,
to teach us the Price of ſo rich a Jewel. *

That we may learn to value every Hour,
and not childiſhly ſpend it on empty Trifles:

Much leſs maliciouſly murther whole Days
in purſuing a Courſe of Sin and Shame.

——Lord! as Thou thus haſt taught my Ignorance,
ſo let thy Grace enable my Weakneſs,

Wiſely to manage the Time Thou lendeſt,
and ſtill preſs on to new degrees of Improvement;

That with my few, but well-ſpent Years,
I may purchaſe to myſelf a bleſs'd Eternity:

And, O Thou Saviour of Mankind! in whoſe indulgent Hands

are both our Time and our Eternity;

Whoſe Providence gives every Minute of our Life,
and governs the fatal Period of our Death,

Make every Evening ſtill provide
to paſs with Comfort that important Hour;

That if I riſe no more to my Acquaintance here,
I may joyfully awake among thy bleſſed Angels,

There to unite my Hymns with theirs,
and join with them in one full Choir ——

Glory be to the Father, and to the Son, and to the
Holy Ghoſt;

As it was in the Beginning, is now, and ever ſhall be,
World without End. *Amen!*

* Note XXVII.

TUESDAY MORNING.

Hymn V.

PRAISE, O my Soul, the gracious Hand
    That brought me to this Light;
That gave his Angels ſtrict Command
To be my Guard this Night!

When I laid down my weary Head,
    And Sleep ſeal'd up my Eye,
They ſtood and watch'd about my Bed,
    And let no Harm come nigh.

Now I am up, they ſtill go on
    And guide me thro' the Day;
They never leave their Charge alone,
    Whate'er befets my Way.

But, O my God! how many Snares
    Lie ſpread before my Feet!
In all my Joys, in all my Cares,
    Some Danger ſtill I meet.

The darling Sin doth oft o'ertake
And on my Weaknefs win;
Sometimes myfelf my Ruin make,
And I o'ertake the Sin.

Save me, O Lord! to Thee I cry,
From whom all Bleffings fpring;
I on thy Grace alone rely,
Thy Praife, thy Glory fing!

MEDITATION XVIII.

" Why do we boaft as if we had not received it ?"

1 Cor. iv. 7.

NOT unto us, O Lord! not unto us,
but unto thy Name be all the Glory. (1)
When we've applied our utmoft Care,
and ufed all our Diligence;
What can we do but look up to Thee,
to fecond our Endeavours by thy Spirit!

(1) Pfalm cxv. 1.

When we've implor'd thy Mercy,
and offered to Thee our deareſt Sacrifice;
What can we do but ſubmit our Hopes,
and await the Event from thy free Goodneſs?
I know, Thyſelf haſt taught me,
unleſs Thou (2) " keep the City, the Watchman wa-
keth but in vain."
I know, and my own Experience tells me,
unleſs Thou reach thine Hand I preſently ſink.
Every Moment of my Day ſubſiſts by Thee,
and every Step I take moves by thy Strength.
But — are we not all thy Creatures, O God,
as helpleſs Children hanging on thy Providence?
Behold, I confeſs, O Lord,
in Thee I live, and move, and have my Being. (3)
Others may tell me the Way I ſhould go,
but Thou alone canſt enable me to walk in it.
Should I preſume to divide thy Grace,
proudly challenging any Share to myſelf—
Thy mighty Truth ſtands up againſt me, (4)
and my own Infirmities plainly confute me.
Shouldſt Thou cloſely examine my Heart,
and aſk who works all good Thoughts in it;

---

(2) Pſal. cxxvii. 1.   (3) Acts xvii. 28.

(4) Eph. ii. 8.——" By Grace ye are ſaved through Faith; and that
not of yourſelves; it is the Gift of God."

Surely I muſt bow down my Head, and humbly ſay,
Nothing am I, O Lord, but what Thou haſt made me,
nothing have I but what Thou haſt given me :
(5) Only my Sins are entirely my own, * which,
O, may thy Grace blot out for ever!
May all Self-preſumption die in me,
and my whole Confidence live only in Thee.
May even my Frailties make me more ſtrong,
and my being nothing (6) teach me to be humble.
So ſhall thy Strength, O Lord, be magnified in my
          Weakneſs,
and thy Mercy triumph in the Relief of my Miſery.

MEDITATION XIX.

" *Altho' the Fig-tree* † *ſhall not bloſſom.*"   Heb. iii. 17.

THUS Man depends, and happy in this Dependance,
did he but know his own true Intereſt.
    Let me then ſit down in Peace,
reſting ſecurely in the Boſom of Providence.

(5) Rom. vii. 18.   * Note XXVIII.
(6) 2 Cor. vi. 10.—" Having nothing, yet poſſeſſing all Things."
                † Note XXIX.

Every Accident may improve a Virtue,
and every Virtue is a ftep of approach towards God.

Whate'er befalls, let this be my conftant Rule,
— " to provide for the future life, and be contented
with the prefent."

Shall I not patiently accept a little Evil,
from Him who has given me fo much Good?

Shall the being without fome one thing I need not,
more fenfibly affect me than the having all I need?

Ungrateful that I am! the common Benefits which
all enjoy,
deferve the Thankfgivings of a whole Life:

But for thofe high fupernatural Bleffings,
the Son of God to redeem, and Heaven to reward me;

What fhall I fay! — If I would fpeak of them,
they are more than I am able (7) to exprefs.

Can I then yet complain
that others are more profperous than I?

Should I not rather look on the Miferies of others,
and blefs our God who has preferved me from them?

'Tis but interpreting the worft Condition well,
to find Motives enow for Gratitude to God:

'Tis but interpreting the beft Condition frowardly,
to find Defects enow to make myfelf miferable.

(7) Pfalm xl. 5.

F

Would Man humbly adore his Maker,
he would readily trust him to rule his own World :
And could he decypher the Character of his Decrees,
he would read in each Syllable a perfect Harmony.
Suffer me not then, O God, to follow my private
Spirit,
lest I create to myself a voluntary Misery;
Still let me construe the Afflictions Thou sendest,
as meant to correct, not to destroy me;
To prevent some Sin, or beget some Virtue:
— for when I no longer need Afflictions,
Thou wilt remove either me, or them.
Meanwhile, O gracious Father,
make me patiently await thy Time!
Make me rejoice that my Lot is in thine Hand,
but ——O let thy Mercy choose favorably for me!
Dispose as Thou pleasest my Condition here ——
only my Portion hereafter — let *That* be blessed !

TUESDAY EVENING.

H y m n   VI.

BLESSED, O Lord, be thy wife Grace
That governs all my Day,
And to the Night affigns its Place,
To reft me in my Way!

If Works the lab'ring Hand impair,
Or Thoughts the ftudious Mind;
Both are confider'd by thy Care,
Both fit Refrefhment find :

Fit to relieve their prefent State,
And guide them to the next;
While they are taught to meditate
This plain and ufeful Text;

" As every Night lays down my Head,
" And Morning opes mine Eyes;
" So fhall the Duft be once my Bed,
" And fo I hope to rife :

" To rife — and fee th' all-beauteous Light
" Spring from the Fount divine;
" Not to be check'd by any Night,
" But clear for ever fhine."

———————

MEDITATION   XX.

" *When thy Judgments are in the Earth, the Inhabitants*
of the World will learn Righteoufnefs." Ifa. xxvi. 9.

SPEAK no more proudly, vain Duft,
nor provoke the living God!
Remember how the Clouds rain'd Fire and Brimftone,
and buried whole Cities in their own Afhes:
Remember how the Deluge o'erfpread the World,
and fwept away impenitent Mankind.
Reflect, and afk the Caufe,
proclaim it to the bold Offender;
Tell him 'twas Sin, and fuch as his,
that drew from Heaven fo fwift Deftruction.
——Can I repeat thefe amazing Truths,
and not tremble at the Wrath of JUSTICE?
Can I confider the End of Sinners,
and ftill go on in the Ways of Sin?

Even while I fpeak thy Praifes, Lord,
my very Duty fhould fear before Thee.

What fhould corrupted Nature then do,
when it fees itfelf ready to offend Thee!

What fhould a guilty Confcience do,
when it feels itfelf ruin'd by offending Thee!

Strike Thou my Heart, O infinite Majefty,
with an awful Reverence of thy great Name!

Correct my many Levities into a pious Sadnefs,
and bend my proud Spirit to thy Will!

Still may my Confcience cry within me,
" dareft thou commit this Evil, and fin againft God?"

O forbid it, gracious Lord,
and make thy Judgments on others Mercies to me!

MEDITATION XXI.

" Mercy and Truth are met together — Righteoufnefs and
Peace have kiffed each other." Pfal. lxxxv. 10.

HE, who is thus infinite in Power to punifh,
is alfo infinite in Goodnefs to fave.

How often have I broken his Comands! —
yet ftill his Earth fuftains and ferves me.

How often have I abus'd his Fulnefs of Bread!
yet ftill his Clouds fhow'r Plenty upon me.

     Only the ambitious Angels find no Forgivenefs,
becaufe their Obftinacy refufes to feek it. *

     But, O the Excefs of Bounty vouchfafed to Man!
The King of Heaven humbled himfelf
to dwell upon the Earth;

     Leading a poor laborious Life,
and fuffering a painful ignominious Death;

     To teach Man how to live, and die,
to labour, and fuffer for his own Happinefs.

     —Thy Mercies, O Lord, are over all thy Works,
and this above all thy Mercies!

MEDITATION XXII.

" *The Eyes of all wait upon Thee.*" Pfal. cxlv. 15.

HOW ingrateful am I!
    how ftrangely infenfible to my manifeft Duty!
     Every Creature hears thy Voice, O God!
and lives by thy Rule, but I.

* Note XXX,

The Sun obferves his conftant Rifing,
and fets exactly at his appointed Time.

The Sun ftands ftill at thy Command,
the Sun goes back to obey thy Voice — (8)

And yet feeks no Reward,
nor expects to be placed in a higher Heaven.

But Man, who looks for fuch glorious Promifes,
and aims no lower than the Heav'n of Heavens;

Shall He, redeemed by the Blood of Jefus,
neglect fo great Salvation?

Shall he flight Him, whofe kind Intent
is to draw him to his Love?

Shall he defpife fo generous a love,
whofe only effect is to make him happy?

—— May thy Will, O Lord, be my only Rule,
thy Hand my only Guide!

MEDITATION XXIII.

" The Day is thine, the Night alfo is thine;
Thou haft prepared the Light and the Sun." Pf. lxxiv. 16.

'TWAS not alone to make the Day,
that Thou, O Lord, didft make the Sun;

(8) Jofhua x. 12.

But to teach Man thefe pious Leffons,
and to write them plainly as its own bright Beams;
  " So let your Light fhine forth to others; (9)
" fo your Charity warm their Coldnefs."
  Thus when they fay — " You are under a Cloud—"
I will, like the Sun, be really above it :
  And, tho' I appear fometimes eclips'd,
or e'en extinguifh'd in a Night of Sorrow,
  Still will I fhine to myfelf and Thee,
and ftill go on in the Ways of Light :
  Still, like the regular Sun, unchangedly expect
the appointed Periods of Bright and Dark :
  Only in this we difagree — and —
— blefs'd be my God who made the Difference !
  Not like the Sun, that every Night goes down,
and muft at laft be quite put out ; (1)
  When I have finifh'd here my Courfe,
and feem to fet to this dark Earth ;
  I hope to rife and fet no more, *
but fhine perpetually in a brighter Heaven.

(9) St Matt. v. 16.   (1) St Mark xiii. 24, 31.
* Note XXXI.

WEDNESDAY MORNING.

H y m n VII.

LORD! I again lift up mine Eyes,
  And leave my fluggifh Bed;
But why I wake, and why I rife,
Comes feldom in my Head.

Is it to fweat and toil for Wealth,
Or fport my Time away;
That Thou preferv'ft me ftill in Health,
And giv'ft me this new Day?

No, no — unfkilful Soul — not fo,
Be not deceiv'd with Toys;
Thy Lord's Commands more wifely go,
And aim at higher Joys.

They bid me 'wake to feek new Grace,
And fome frefh Virtue gain;
They call me up to mend my Pace,
Till I the Prize attain.

G

That glorious Prize for which all run,
Who wifely fpend their Breath;
Who, when this weary Life is done,
Are fure of Reft in Death.

Not fuch a Reft as here they prove,
Difturb'd with Cares and Fears:
But endlefs Joy, and Peace, and Love,
Unmix'd with Grief and Tears.

Glory to Thee, O bounteous Lord,
Who giv'ft to all Things Breath!
Glory to Thee, Eternal Word,
Who fav'ft me by thy Death!

Glory, O blefled Spirit, to Thee,
Who fill'ft my Soul with Love!
Glory to all the facred Three,
Who reign one God above!

MEDITATION XXIV.

" *Depart from me, ye curfed.*" St Matt. xxv. 41.

WHY doft thou laugh, unhappy Wretch,
and weary thyfelf in the Ways of Sin?

Awake, and chafe the Dream away,
that deludes thy fick Head with empty Vanities!
  Whither, alas! will thy Soul be hurried, when, de-
    fpairing,
thou figh'ft forth thy laft faint Breath?
  Thither — where Memory will renew thy Sorrows,
where the Worm of Confcience dieth not. *
  At the laft great Day, the Impenitent
will call to the Mountains to fall on them,
and to the Hills to cover them:
  —Nothing fhall fall on them but the Wrath of God,
nothing fhall cover them but their own Confufion.
  Then will each Vice, produced of its own Corruption,
receive its proper Punifhment.
  Thus wilt thou, miferable Sinner,
wail forth thy late Remorfe——
    " What now avail the wanton Pleafures
  " I fo eagerly purfued!
    " What Comfort to me now the Opinion of the
      " World,
  " and the faithlefs Riches I fo highly priz'd!
    " They all are vanifh'd as a Cloud,
  " and nothing left me but Regret!"
  O, fad Expectance of a diffolute Life!
O, dreadful Confequence of an impenitent Death!

* Note XXXII.

G 2

For ever to long for what cannot be enjoy'd;
for ever to fuffer what cannot be avoided !·

—— Blefs'd be thy Providence, O God,
that with fuch tender Care forewarns me of my Danger!

O ! fave me from the Sinner's Doom !
Save me for thy Mercy's Sake !

Make me fearful to do, what, when done,
will make me miferable to fuffer ! †

MEDITATION XXV.

—— *" not to me only, but to all
them that love his appearing."* 2 Tim. iv. 8.

WHY doft thou mourn, thou Child of Light,
    to whom belong fuch glorious Promifes ;
· Who feed'ft on the Fruits of Piety,
the continual feaft of a good Confcience ;
    Who tafteft already the Sweetnefs of Hope,
hereafter to be fatisfied with the Fulnefs of Joy ?
    There — where freed from Temptation,
no more to be crofs'd by thyfelf or others —

† Note XXXIII.

There every Virtue fhall wear its proper Crown,
and fhine in a Diadem fit for its own Head ;
  There fhalt thou rejoice in a glorified Body,
in the Perfections of an enlarged Soul ;
  In the Society of Saints and Angels,
in the Prefence of thy God and Saviour.
  Then wilt thou blefs the true Friend that reproved
        thee,
and the charitable Hand that led thee to Happinefs.
  O, fweet Expectance of a pious Life !
O, happy Confequence of an holy Death !
  For ever to be free from what can afflict,
for ever to enjoy all that can delight !
  —— Blefs'd be thy Providence, O God,
that, with fo large a Bounty, invites me to Happinefs—
  Engaging, by the Means moft apt to take me,
a Love of Myfelf and mine own Intereft !
  As Thou haft prepared fuch Joys for me,
I implore thy Grace to prepare me for them :
  Still let me labour, ftill let me fuffer ; *
my Troubles are fhort, my Joys eternal.

* Note XXXIV.

MEDITATION XXVI.

*" What will it profit a Man to gain the whole World,
and lose his own Soul? or what shall a Man give in Ex-
change for his Soul?"* St Mark viii. 36.

COME, now, my Soul, and choose,
 for Life and Death are set before thee : (1)
Choose, while thy Lord allows thee Day,
lest the Night of Darkness o'ertake thy Neglect.
 Choose, but remember an Eternity is concern'd ;
examine well e'er thou resolve.
 Call all the Pleasures of the World before thee,
and look if any of them be worth thy seeking.
 Dost thou expect Quiet by enjoying them,
or Happiness by their Procurement?
 Will they protect thee at the Hour of Death,
or plead thy Cause at the Day of Judgment?
 " Ah ! no — they but deceive me with their Smiles,
" which I too oft have prov'd by dear Experience.
 " 'Tis Heav'n alone that can satisfy my Soul.
 " Turn away mine Eyes then, O Lord, lest they
  " behold Vanity,
" and quicken me in thy Law ! " (2)

(1) Deut. xxx. 15.   (2) Psal. cxix. 37.

Here we move flowly in the Dark,
led on by the Argument of Things not feen: (3)
  But did we clearly fee what we *fay* we believe,
foon fhould we turn unto God.

  Could we difcern the Damned in their Torments,
how fhould we fear to follow them in their Sins —
which plung'd them into endlefs Mifery!

  Could we but fee the Glories of the Bleffed,
how carefully fhould we ftudy to imitate their Virtues—
which led them to endlefs Happinefs!

  Nay — my Soul — could'ft thou now tafte
the Joys of Heav'n, what Exercife on Earth
for thy Life of Trial?

  Rather let me fay — did our Faith but firmly believe
the Truths we every Day recite;
  What would we not do to attain thofe Joys!
What would we not do to efcape thofe Sorrows!

  Would the Pardon of an Injury be too hard a Law,
or the making Reftitution too dear a Price?

  Yet is all this as fure as if we faw it,
and would move us as much if we *vitally* believ'd. *

  If we confider'd what a Chriftian *muft* believe,
we could not live fo like Heathens as we do.

  Pity, O Lord, my Frailty!
and fuffer not my Blindnefs to be my Ruin!

(3) 2 Cor. iv. 18.   * Note XXXV.

Supply my Want of Sight by a lively Faith,
and ftrengthen my Faith by thy Grace!

Make me choofe wifely, and purfue my Choice,
then will I ferve Thee in Fear, and rejoice before Thee
in Hope and Love!

H y m n   VIII.

AND do I then believe
   There is a Life to come,
When all the World fhall fummon'd be
   To take their final Doom?

Is there a Heav'n, indeed,
   To crown the Innocent?
Is there a Hell and horrid Pains
   The Wicked to torment?

Are thefe eternal too,
   And never to have end?
Shall never thefe Delights decay,
   Thofe Sorrows never mend?

God's Word proclaims it true;
   And fure moft true it is:
And yet I live, as if there were
   Nothing fo falfe as this.

O quicken, Lord, my Faith
   Of thefe great Joys and Fears;
And let the laft Day's Trumpet be
   Still founding in my Ears!

H

Still make this glorious Hope
Shine bright before mine Eyes:
—I shall at last go up to meet
My Saviour in the Skies.

MEDITATION XXVII.

" Lord, save us, we perish!" St Matt. viii. 25.

HOW secure and quiet they live,
    whom thy Grace, O Lord! preserves in Inno-
    cence!

The Spirits of their Fancies run calm and even,
and ebb and flow, in obedience to Reason:

Their Day passeth smoothly over their Heads,
peaceful, and silent as the Shadow of a Dial.

Not so, a Life subject to Humour,
and the Rule of varying Passions,

Which often engage us in contentions,
embittering our Lives with Strife and Envy;

Inmates, that quarrel among themselves, *
raising a war in our own Bosoms:

* Note XXXVI.

If they agree, and in one Defire fucceed,
feldom do they produce the expected Content:
When they delight our Tafte,
they moft undo us, by feeding our Difeafe.
——Lord, fave me, I perifh!
awake, and with thy Mercy refcue thy Servant!
Calm Thou the Tempeft of my Soul!
then fhall I return to my former Peace:
Peace with the Bad, by bearing their Injuries; *
Peace with the Good, by conforming to their Virtues:
Peace with myfelf, by fubduing Senfe to Reafon;
and—with Thee, by improving Reafon with Religion.

———

MEDITATION . XXVIII.

" *Then He arofe, and rebuked the Winds and the Sea;
and there was a great Calm.*" St Matt. viii. 26.

LORD, as thine All-wife Providence feems to
fleep fometimes,
and permits the Storm to grow high and loud;

* Note XXXVII.

H 2

Yet never faileth to relieve thy Servants,
who faithfully call on Thee in their Day of Trial;
So let thine hand still bear me up,
when I am preſſed by Temptation.

Leave me not, then, to my natural Infirmities,
leſt the Enemy prevail againſt me :
Forſake not my fallen Miſery,
leſt I lie groveling on the Earth :
Suffer not my Frailties to become Habits,
leſt I die impenitent, and periſh for ever !

Deliver me, O Lord, from the occaſions of Sin,
and the Importunities of ſuch as delight in Folly !
Deliver me from the Snare of enticing Company,
and the dangerous Infection of ill Example ! *

(1) " Set a watch before mine Eyes, and keep the
" Door of my Lips ! "

Govern my Senſes, and order each Motion of my
Heart and Fancy !

Perfect, O dear Redeemer, the work Thou haſt begun in me ;
and make my Paſſions Servants of thy Grace !

Convert my rude Anger into a Severity againſt myſelf,
and a temperate Zeal for the good of others !

Let Thy Charity poſſeſs my Soul !

And——O ! Thou Fountain of Bounty !
that flow'ſt ſo freely with perpetual Bleſſings,

* Note XXXVIII.　　　　　(1) Pſalm cxli. 3.

Let every Day I receive of Thee,
ftill fet apart fome portion of itfelf,
  To meditate thine infinite Mercies,
and rejoice in thy glorious Rewards;
  Mercies, that give me all I have;
and Rewards, that referve for me all I can wifh!

MEDITATION XXIX.

" So teach us to number our Days, that we may apply our Hearts unto wifdom." Pf. xc. 12.

I Am nearer my Grave,
  and all the World is older by a Day.
  So much is the Portion of the wicked reduc'd,
and their time of Punifhment brought nearer:
  So much are the Sufferings of the patient diminifh'd,
and their Hopes of Deliverance encreas'd.
  They, who have fpent this Day in Sin,
find all their Thoughts now vanifh like a Dream:
  All's paft, but a Fear of Punifhment;
the beft that can follow is a bitter Repentance.
  But they, who have wifely beftow'd their time,
and made another Step towards Heaven,

Advance to meet their Joys, which increafe
as they draw nearer, till they unite in Death. †
—— O! Thou blefs'd Author of Man's Hopes!
inftruct me in this Truth, and let every Evening renew it on my Mind:
“ The things of this World are of little Import,
“ fince its Joys and Griefs laft only for a Time;
“ But the future State concerns me truly,
“ where Life and Death endure for ever."

Meditation XXX.

" The Night cometh, when no man can work."

St John ix. 4.

WE are nearer the End of our Life;
but are we nearer the object for which we
live?
What Good haft Thou done, my Soul, to-day?
Have I avoided any known Temptation;
or refifted, when I could not avoid?
Have I interrupted my cuftomary faults,
and check'd the Vices I am moft inclin'd to?

† Note XXXIX.

Have I improv'd the Opportunities of doing good,
which the Mercy of Providence offered to me?

Did I contrive Occafions of Improvement
for thofe with whom I convers'd?

Alas! dread Lord! what do I fee,
when I ferioufly look into myfelf!

When I reflect upon my former years;
nay, even the Follies of this one Day!

So many Hours mif-fpent in nothing;
fo many abus'd in worfe than nothing!

————Pardon, O meek Redeemer! the Evil I have
done,
and fupply the Good I have omitted!

Make me to watch,
left my future time flide unprofitably away!

Make me daily to ftudy
the Knowledge of myfelf and Thee:

Myfelf, to correct my many Infirmities;
Thee, to adore thine Infinite Perfections!

MEDITATION XXXI.

——— " *not I, but the Grace of God which was with me.*" 1 Cor. xv. 10.

LITTLE is the Good I do;
and even that little is deriv'd from God.
Great are the Evils I commit,
and all to be charg'd upon myfelf.
Tell me, my Soul; and let not Pride* deny the
Truth:
Could we have fav'd ourfelves from Temptation
without the Help of God?
Could we have accomplifh'd any one pious Purpofe,
unlefs his Hand had blefs'd the Endeavour?
No! to Thyfelf, O Lord! be all the Praife,
if thy Creature have done any Good:
To Thee alfo be the Glory,
if I have not committed the greateft Sins.†
Thine Hand directs me to do well;
and the fame blefs'd Hand reftrains me from Ill.
'Tis not in Man to efteem unfeen Joys,
and defpife the Flatteries of this deceitful World;

* Note XL.   † Note XLI.

'Tis not the Work of corrupted Nature,
to mortify Senfe, and patiently to bear Afflictions:
Of myfelf, I am inclin'd to none of thefe;
but the Grace of God enables me to all.

THURSDAY MORNING.

H y m n IX.

" COME UNTO ME, ALL YE THAT LABOUR
AND ARE HEAVY LADEN, AND I WILL RE-
FRESH YOU." St Matt. xi. 28.

I Come! renewed from above
With loyal Faith, and humble Love!
I come, O Lord! I bow to Thee,
Whom heav'nly Love bow'd low'r for me.

Faith is my Eye, Faith Strength affords,
To keep Pace with thofe gracious Words;
And Words more kind, more fure than they,
Love could not think, Truth could not fay.

O dear Memorial of that Death
Which ftill furvives and gives us Breath!
Man's Bread of Life! O may'ft Thou be
My Food, my Joy, and All to me!

I come, O Lord! my Hopes increase:
Give me my Portion in thy Peace.
Come, hidden (1) Life! and that long Day,
For which I languish, come away!

When this dry Soul thine Eyes shall see,
And drink the unseal'd Source of Thee;
When Glory's Sun Faith's Shade shall chace,
And for thy Veil give me thy Face.

M E D I T A T I O N XXXII.

———— " it *shall bruise thy Head, and thou shalt*
bruise his Heel." Genesis iii. 15.

UNHAPPY Man! at first created just,
     as every Work comes fair from the Hands of God:
   At first endow'd with Dominion over the Earth,
and, which is more, with Dominion over himself,
   At first not only made sole Lord of Paradise,
but Heir of the Heav'n of Heavens ————

(1) " Your Life is hid with Christ in God." Col. iii. 3.

I 2

All this was loft by one rafh Act; *
—difobeying the Law of thy wife Creator.
    All this we lofe by thy Tranfgreffion,
which brought in Sin, and Death, and Mifery:
    Our Bodies are deprav'd by thy Diftemper,
and our very Souls partake of the Corruption: †
    Our Senfe rebels againft Reafon,
and both confpire againft the Will of God.
    Soon did Ignorance o'erfpread the World,
and Error and Vice poffefs Mankind.
    The Law they obey'd was their Appetite,
and the God they worfhipp'd the Work of their own
        Hands.
    Even the felected People, the favoured Nation
of the Almighty Providence;
    They, who had feen the Sea divide,
and ftand on each Side as a Wall to defend them:
    E'en they forgat their great Deliverer,
and fet up for their God, the God of their Enemies.
    They could not worfhip what they did not fee,
they muft have Gods to go before them. (2)
    Thus lay the miferable World all cover'd with
        Darkuefs,
and the thick Mift of grofs Idolatry.

* Note XLII.   † Note XLIII.
(2) Exod. xxxii. 1.

This mov'd thy Pity, gracious Lord!
(who oft art found by thofe that feek Thee not)
This mov'd thy Pity to undertake our Relief — *
—Thou didft come and dwell amongft us;
That as our Nature us'd to worfhip what it faw,
† we fhould now fee Him whom we might fafely
worfhip.
When Thou didft leave our World for Heav'n,
to prepare a Place for thy faithful Followers;
Thou didft not leave us comfortlefs,
nor wholly forfake our Earth:
For ftill Thou doft fend thine Holy Spirit,
and thus give thyfelf to thy true Difciples.

MEDITATION XXXIII.

" The Bread of God is He which cometh down from
Heaven, and giveth Life unto the World." St John vi. 33.

WHERE, O Thou boundlefs Ocean of Charity,
where will thine overflowing Streams ftay
their Courfe!

* Note XLIV.   † Note XLV.

We, and our Ingratitude ftrive to oppofe Thee,
but nothing can refift thine Almighty Goodnefs.

When thy falfe Friend fought to betray,
and deliver Thee into the Hands of impious Men ;

Thou meekly didft fubdue their Malice
by thy Bounty ;

Then didft Thou firft (3) invite all. the World
to a Feaft of Love :

Wherein Thou art the Life, the Strength,
the Comfort of our Souls.

A Feaft of Peace and Love,
to which Thou thus invit'ft us,

" Come to me, ye that labour for Holinefs,
" and are opprefs'd under the Weight of your Sins!

" Come to me, ye that hunger after Righteoufnefs,
" and thirft to drink at the Well of Life !

" Come ! and I will refrefh you ! "

MEDITATION XXXIV,

" *If any Man thirft, let him come unto me and drink.*"
St John vii. 37.

THUS doth our gracious Lord invite: and fhall I go?
Shall a Sinner dare to approach his Table ?

(3) " The *fame* Night that he was betrayed." 1 Cor. ii. 23.

Thus He invites, and fhall I not go!
Shall I prefume to refufe his Call!
  'Rife then, my Soul, and leave the World behind
    thee,
'rife to falute thy Lord!
  But — am I dreft like a Friend of the Bridegroom?
May I fafely go to this Marriage-feaft?
  Have I confider'd how pure that Soul fhould be,
which afpires to an Union with its God?

  Affift me, O Lord, in examining my Heart!
Cleanfe me from my fecret (4) Sins!

  How unworthy am I of this divine Sacrament!
  Yet am I call'd by Him who has a Right to command;
by Him who fees, and pities my Mifery.

  He bids me come, and will receive me!
  " I will go then into his Tabernacle,
  " and fall low on my Knees before his Footftool." (5)
  There will I confefs, and bewail my Sins,
which brought a Saviour from Heav'n, and nail'd him
    to a Crofs.

—Fill me, O Lord, with Faith, and Hope, and Charity;
and ftrengthen me with thy Grace!
  Make me fruitful in holy Thoughts, Words, and
    Actions!

---

(4) Pfal. xix. 12.   (5) Pfal. cxxxii. 7.

Then wilt Thou accept my Sacrifice of Praife,
when I faithfully commemorate the Sacrifice of thy
Death.

THURSDAY EVENING.

H Y M N   X.

FAIN would my Thoughts fly up to Thee,
Thy Peace, O Lord! to find;
But when I offer, ftill the World
Lays Clogs upon my Mind.

Sometimes I climb a little Way,
And thence look down below :
How *nothing* there do all things feem
That here make fuch a Shew !

Then round about I turn mine Eyes,
To feaft my hungry Sight ;
I meet with Heav'n in every thing,
In ev'ry thing Delight.

I fee thy Wifdom ruling all,
And joyfully admire;
I fee myfelf among fuch Hopes
As fet my Heart on fire.

When I have thus triumph'd awhile,
And think to build my Neft,
Some crofs Conceit comes flutt'ring by,
And interrupts my Reft.

Then to the Earth again I fall,
And from my low Duft cry—
'Twas not my Wing, O Lord! but thine
That rais'd me up fo high.

And now, my God! whether I rife,
Or ftill lie down in Duft;
Both I fubmit to thy blefs'd Will,
In both on Thee I truft.

Guide Thou my Way, who art Thyfelf
My everlafting End;
That every Step, or fwift or flow,
Still to Thyfelf may tend!

K

MEDITATION XXXV.

" Repent, for the Kingdom of Heav'n is at hand."
St Matt. iv. 17.

O Lord! when I reflect upon these Words—
" Repent—for the Kingdom of Heav'n is at
hand ".—

When I consider they were the first which Thou
didst preach,

the chosen Text of the Eternal Wisdom;

Stricken with the Importance of the Duty,

I'm deeply affected with the Power of the Motive.

If I feel not the Truth of this last Sentence,

but repeat it only as a Form of Devotion;

Forgive the Deceitfulness of my Heart!

and make me *think*, as well as *say* my Prayers!

Make me apply those searching Words unto myself;

" Repent, for the Kingdom of Heav'n is at hand; "

Repent, for the Kingdom of Heav'n

depends upon thy Repentance.

Unhappy that I am, who cannot live without Sin,

nor hope for Pardon without due Repentance!

I cannot repent without the Grace of God,

nor obtain his Grace but by his own free Gift. (1)

(1) Rom. ii. 4.—2 Tim. ii. 25.

O, my Saviour, who cameſt, not to call the Right-
eous,
but ſuch as I am to Repentance,
Since I am not ſtrong enough to be perfeᔆly innocent,
make me ſo humble, as to be truly penitent!

Deliver me from the Puniſhments I deſerve,
and from the Sins which deſerve thoſe Puniſhments!

Teach me that ſafe and eaſy Method
of cenſuring myſelf, to be acquitted by Thee!

Every night let me ſit as an impartial Judge,
and call before me all my Day:
Let me ſeverely examine every Thought and Word,
and ponder each Deed and each Omiſſion:
Imploring for the paſt the Mercy of Heaven,
and for the time to come the ſame unbounded Mercy.

If perchance I find ſome things well done,
when weigh'd with the Allowances indulg'd our Frailty;
Let me give all the Glory to God,
and beg his Grace to continue and improve them.

His is the Hand that ſows the Seed;
his the Bleſſing that gives the Increaſe.

Thus let me once a Day look home,
and ſtriᔆly examine the State of my Soul:
Still let me write at the foot of my Account,
——*Reconciled to God, and in Charity with the world.*——

Then go to Bed with a quiet Confcience, *
and fall afleep in Peace and Hope.

MEDITATION XXXVI.

" *Ifaac went out to meditate in the Fields at Even-
tide.*" Gen. xxiv. 63.

HOW fhall I gain this Favour,
to find my God alone?
I will feek Him in the Silence of Retirement,
and unfold before Him all my Wants:
I will feek Him while He may be found, (1)
and humbly afk the charity of his Counfel.
Where, O my God! is Happinefs? †
And what fhall I do to obtain it?
Nature already hath thus far taught me,
in all I undertake to feek mine own Good.
But unlefs Thou vouchfafe to inftruct,
and fhew me true Felicity;
I fear I may miftake that Good,
and fet up an Idol inftead of Thee.

* Note XLVI.   (1) Pfalm xxxii. 7.
† Note XLVII.

— HEAR THOU THE ETERNAL WISDOM!
" Seek ye firſt the Kingdom of God,
" and all things needful ſhall be added unto you." (1)
Theſe, my Lips confeſs, are excellent Truths;
but when ſhall my Life confeſs them?
When ſhall I ſubdue my Paſſions, or guide them ſo,
that they may draw me to thy Light?
While they are mine, I cannot govern them:
Behold—here I offer them, O God, unto Thee!
Check Thou their Motions by thy Grace,
leſt they hurry me beyond the Bounds of Duty:
Wean Thou my Heart from the Follies of the World,
and increaſe my Deſire for Heavenly Joys:
Where'er I am in this inconſtant State,
ſtill let mine inward Eye look up to Thee;
Still may I long for that happy Day, .
when I ſhall ſee, and no more darkly (2) believe,
That Thou, O Lord!
art my God, and All Things.

(1) St Matt. vi. 33.   (2) 1 Cor. xiii. 12.

FRIDAY MORNING.

H y m n XI.

I Will adore the King of Love,
  And King of Suff'rings too;
For Love it was that brought Him down,
And fet Him here in Woe.

Love drew Him from his Paradife,
Where Flow'rs, that fade not, grow;
And planted him in our poor Duft,
Among us Weeds below.

Here for a time this heav'nly Plant
Fairly grew up and thriv'd;
Diffus'd its Fragrance all around,
And all in Sweetnefs liv'd.

But envious Frofts, and furious Storms,
So long, fo fiercely chide,
This tender Flow'r at laft bow'd down
Its bruifed Head, and dy'd.

O narrow Thoughts, and narrow Speech,
Your Poverty confefs!

A Saviour's Life, a Saviour's Death,
How faintly you exprefs!

May He, who from a Virgin Root
Made this fair Flow'r to fpring,
Help me to raife both Heart and Voice,
And with more Spirit fing—

     " To Father, Son, and Holy Ghoft,
     " One undivided Three,
     " All higheft Praife, all humbleft Thanks,
     " Now and for ever be! "

MEDITATION XXXVII.

" *Being found in fafhion as a Man, He humbled him-felf for us, and became obedient unto Death, even the Death of the Crofs.*" Philipp. ii. 8.

WHO, that remembers the Afflictions of his Sa-
        viour,
can repine at his own Sufferings?
    E'en from the Cradle to the Crofs, how little do we
        read
of Glad and Profperous, how much of Pain and Grief!

" We hid, as it were, our Faces from him : (1)

" He was defpifed, and we efteemed Him not.

" He was oppreffed, and He was afflicted;

" yet He opened not his Mouth: He is brought as

" a Lamb to the Slaughter; and as a Sheep

" before her Shearers is dumb, fo He opened not his
    " Mouth. "

Thus were his Sufferings defcrib'd,

Ages before he was fent into the World.

Can I then complain of Suffering,

when the King of Glory did nothing but fuffer?

I wear the Badge of a crucified Saviour,

and fhall I fhrink back at every Crofs I meet?

I believe in a Lord who was crown'd with Thorns,

and fhall I abide to tread on nothing but Rofes?

I fee Thee, Jefus, humble and meek,

and fhall thy Servant be proud and infolent?

I fee Thee going about poor and unregarded,

and fhall thy Difciple ftrive only to be rich and
    efteemed?

Thy charitable Labours were malicioufly flandered,

and fhall not my Faults have the Patience to be re-
    prov'd?

O! how unlike am I to that blefs'd Original,

which defcended from Heaven to become my Pattern!

(1) Ifaiah, liii.

———Pity my Infirmities, O Lord,
and ſtrengthen me with thy Grace!
    Endue me with the heavenly Virtues
of Faith, and Hope, and invincible Charity;
    That I may firmly and conſtantly oppoſe
whatever ſtands in my way to Heaven!
    Since I muſt ſuffer as a Chriſtian,
and deſerve it as a Sinner;
    Aſſiſt me to bear it
as becometh thy Servant!

MEDITATION XXXVIII.

"*He is the Propitiation for our Sins.*" 1 John i. 2.

O Saviour! when I conſider what Thou ſufferedſt
        for me,
and what I have done againſt Thee,
    I am amaz'd at thy Goodneſs,
and confounded at my own Vileneſs!
    My Sins were the Cauſe of thy Death,
and yet I permit them ſtill to live in me.

L

But — Thou canft forgive more than I can offend;
yet Thou wilt not forgive, unlefs I *fear* to offend:

Unlefs I feek to Thee for Peace and Reconciliation,
and humble myfelf in thy holy Prefence.

Wherefore, behold, O Lord, I fall down before Thee,
and implore thy Forgivenefs!

All I can offer thine offended Majefty,
is an Eye bath'd in Tears, and a penitent Heart,
broken with Contrition.

And yet even this firm Refolution of Amendment
I muft firft beg of Thee. *

O Saviour of Mankind! who freely pardoneft all
that truly turn to Thee!

Who giveft Repentance to all that afk, (1)
and inviteft all to afk by promifing to give.

Make me fearch diligently for my fecret Sins,
and ftrive to caft them out by Prayer and Self-denial!

Correct them with the Works of Repentance,
that their Stains may be cleanfed by thy Blood. (2)

* Note XLVIII.

(1) Compare Acts xi. 18. with Rom. ii. 4.

(2) 1 John i. 7.

MEDITATION XXXIX.

" God forbid that I should glory, save in the Cross of our Lord Jesus Christ." Gal. vi. 14.

SHALL I rejoice To-day, shall I not mourn
at the Funeral of our Redeemer?
Such was the Excess of his Goodness,
as to derive Joys for us from his own Sorrows.
He forbade his Followers to weep for Him,
referving to Himself the Shame and Grief.
But whither, O Lord, do thy Compaffions carry
Thee,
muft Thou fuffer for us the Pains of Death!
Yes — Thy Mercy ftill obferv'd fome Wants in our
Nature,
as yet unfupplied ——
Thou faweft our too great Fondnefs for Life,
needed thy parting with it to reconcile us to Death.
Thou faweft our Fear of Sufferings could no Way
be abated,
but by freely undergoing them in thine own Perfon,

O bleffed Lord! whofe Grace alone begins, and ends,
and perfects all our Hopes!

To Thee we owe more than ourfelves,
for repairing the Ruins of our fallen Nature.

Thy Power to create faid but a Word,
and inftantly Man became a living Soul:

But thy Wifdom to redeem us,
both fpake much, and wrought more, and fuffered
     moft of all;

— Yea, even the Crofs — where, after three long
     Hours

of Grief, and Shame, and Pain;

Thou meekly bow'dft thy fainting Head,
and, in an Agony of Prayer, yieldedft up the Ghoft.

So fets the Sun in a Cloud,
and leaves our Earth in Darknefs;

But goes to fhine in another 'World,
and foon returns, and brings us Light.

But Thou doeft more, O Lord!
thy very Darknefs brought us Light;

For by thy Death,
we are made to live.

——Can I then remember thy Death,
and not be convinc'd of my Duty to Thee?

Can my cold Heart recount thy Sufferings,
and not be warm'd by the Love that fuffer'd?

Can I believe my Salvation coft Thee fo dear,
and live as if to be fav'd were not worth my Pains?
    Ungrateful that I am ! how do I flight
the Kindnefs of my God !
    How carelefsly comply
with his gracious Defign !

FRIDAY EVENING.

H y m n   XII.

L O N G had the World in Darknefs fate,
    Till Chrift, in all his Father's Light,
Began to dawn from Heav'n's fair Gate,
And diffipate the Clouds of Night.

I too in Darknefs ftill had ftood,
The Slave of Sin, in Death's black Shade ;
But Mercy came, and with his Blood
A gen'ral Ranfom freely paid.

Not all the Malice of the Jews,
Nor Death itſelf, could Him remove;
Still He the bleſs'd Deſign purſues,
And gives his Life to take our Love.

And now, my Lord, my God, my All,
What ſhall I moſt in Thee admire;
That Pow'r which made the World, and ſhall
The World at laſt diſſolve by Fire! (2)

O, no! thy ſtrange Humility,
Thy Wounds, thy Pains, thy Croſs, thy Death;
Theſe ſhall alone my Wonders be,
My Health, my Staff, my Joy, my Breath!

MEDITATION XL.

"*The Words that I ſpeak unto you are Spirit and Life.*"
St John vi. 63.

I Will not, O Lord, ſo ill requite thy Love,
as to renew thy Sufferings by my Sins.

(2) Iſaiah xxxiv. 4.—2 Peter iii. 10, 11, 12.

If I defpife the leaft of thy Servants,
how am I better than Herod who fcorn'd Thee?

If, through Fear, I act againft my Confcience,
how am I better than Pilate who condemn'd Thee?

While I deprive another of his Right,
what do I but diveft Thee of thy Garments?

While I delight in Strife and Schifm,
do I not rend thy feamlefs Coat?

By forfaking thy Will to follow mine own,
do I not choofe a Murtherer before Thee?

By retaining a fharp and bitter Malice,
do I not give Thee Vinegar and Gall to drink?

Do I thus " crucify the Son of God afrefh, (3)
" and put him to an open Shame?"

Are thefe the Thanks, this the Duty,
my Gratitude returns?

But if I have hitherto perfecuted Thee in thy Members, O Lord,

I will mourn my Offences,
And labour to " bring forth Fruits
" meet for Repentance"! (4)

I will afcend the Mount of Calvary,
and affift the pious Jofeph in *uncrucifying* Jefus.

(3) Heb. vi. 6.   (4) St Matt. iii. 8.

Like him we unfasten the Nails,
when we loosen our Affections from cleaving to the
    World :
Like him we cover thy Body,
when our Charity cloaths thy Servants,
    And hides the Infirmities
of thy little ones.

MEDITATION XLI.

" Where your Treasure is, there will your Heart be also."
                 St Matt. vi. 21.

I Will examine the Account of my Time, *
    and sum up the Profit I have made To-day.
What have I gain'd by all I have heard and seen,
since nothing is so barren but may yield some Fruit ?
    Have I cherish'd the Influence of a good Example,
which our gracious Lord presented to excite me ?
    If I have fallen into thoughtless Company,
which so often engages me in Folly ;

* Note XLIX.

Has the Danger increas'd my Care?
Does another's Sin breed Virtue in me? *
  Ah! no! of myself I am cold and languid!
" Quicken me, O Lord, in thy Righteousness." (5)
  Where'er I go, still Sin will follow;
the Sins of others or mine own.
  Where'er I go, still Crosses attend,
and even my Pleasures are tedious unto me.
  Who then has Happiness?
Or, rather, who is in the Way to attain it?
  He that with Patience resolves to suffer †
whate'er his Endeavours are not able to avoid. (1)
  He that with Patience resolves to suffer
what a merciful Father shall send to correct him. ‖
  When I arrive at this,
that Afflictions seem light for the Love of Christ;
  Then shall I find the best Heaven
this Earth can afford;
  And take it as a Pledge
of a better to come.

---

* Note L.   (5) Psal. cxix. 40.

† Note LI.   ‖ Note LII.

(1) See Psal. cxix. 71, and the whole of Ecclef. ii.

M

MEDITATION XLII.

" The very Hairs of your Head are all numbered."

St Matt. x. 30.

WHEN thus retir'd, and fitly difpos'd
        for quiet Thoughts :
Shall the Greatnefs of another moleft my Peace,
or his profp'rous Condition make me repine ?
    Shall I fay in my Heart, had I that fair Eftate,
or, were I entrufted with fo high an Office ;
    I fhould order things more wifely,
for the public Good, and my private Advantage ?
    No : let me rather confider how I manage my own
            Employments,
and fill the Space I occupy in the World.
    When I have Leifure, am I not idle ?
or, fpend my Hours in unprofitable Follies ?
    When bufy, am I not fo too much,
leaving no time to provide for my Soul ?
    Do the Riches I have, make me wife ?
Am I Eyes to the Blind, and Food to the Hungry ?

If poor, am I honeft,
as well as induftrious in my lawful Calling ?
Does my Poverty make me humble ?
Am I charitable in *Thought*, when I cannot be fo in
    Deed ?
Do I in every State give Thanks to Heaven,
and contentedly fubmit to its wife Decrees ?
Can I fay — " O my ador'd Creator !
" I rejoice that my Lot is in thy Hands !
" Thou art All-wifdom, and knoweft my Wants ;
" Thou art All-goodnefs, and delighteft to relieve.
" Under thy Providence I am fafe :
" Whate'er befals, thou guideft it to my Good.
" If Thou wilt have me obfcure and low,
" and eat the Bread of Poverty and Affliction : `
" If Thou wilt load my Back with Croffes,
" or embitter my Days with Sicknefs :
" Thy Will, O Lord !
" not mine, be done ! (6)
" Place where Thou pleafeft thine other Favours,
" but fecure to my Soul a Portion in thy Love :
" Caft me not away from thy Prefence (7) for ever,
" nor blot out (8) my Name from the Book of Life !

---

(6) St Luke xxii. 42.   (7) Pfal. li. 11.

(8) Pfal. lxix. 29.—Deut. xxix. 20.

" But, my eternal Hopes, let them remain;
" and ftill grow quicker as they approach to their End."

—— I will lay down my Head in Peace,
and reft, fecure in the Protection of my God.

SATURDAY MORNING.

H y m n XIII.

HARK, my Soul! how every Thing
    Strives to ferve our bounteous King!
Each a double Tribute pays,
Sings its Part, and then obeys.

Nature's fweet and chiefeſt Choir,
Him with chearful Notes admire,
Chanting every Day their Laûds,
While the Grove their Song applauds.

Tho' their Voices lower be,
Streams have too their Melody;
Night and Day they warbling run,
Never paufe, but ſtill ſing on.

All the Flow'rs that gild the Spring
Hither their ſtill Mufic bring:
If Heav'n blefs them, thankful they
Smell more fwect, and look more gay.

Only Man can fcarce afford
This fmall Tribute to his Lord:
Man, on whom his Bounty flows,
All things gives, and nothing owes.

'Wake for fhame, my fluggifh Heart,
,Wake, and gladly fing thy Part!
Learn of Birds, and Streams, and Flow'rs,
How to ufe thy nobler Pow'rs!

Call whole Nature to thy Aid,
Since 'twas HE whole Nature made!
Join in one eternal Song
ALL — who to one God belong!

———————

MEDITATION XLIII.

" *Thou wilt not leave my Soul in Hell, neither wilt*
Thou fuffer thine Holy One to fee Corruption."

Pfal. xvi. 10, compared with Acts ii. 25, 27.

PROSTRATE before thy Tomb, O Lord!
   I confefs my Mifery, and implore thy Mercy!
Peacefully in the Sepulchre thy Body repofed,
and thy Soul — was not left in Hell.

But whither, O Saviour, fhall my Soul go,
encompafs'd with a Body fo frail, and a World fo
    corrupt ?

Whither, but to Thee, the Juftifier of Sinners,
and to thy Grace, the Suftainer of the Weak !

Thy Grace enables the Penitent to perform his
    Refolves —

for, when all's done, thy Grace muft give the Succefs.

Govern me with this thy Grace, O eternal Wifdom !
and direct my Goings in thy Way. (9)

Order every Chance to prevent my Falling,
and ftill lead me on to a happy End !

If I muft needs undergo the Trial,
and engage Man's fubtle Enemy :

Strengthen me, O Lord !
to perfevere with Courage ;

That I may never be wanting
in Fidelity to Thee.

MEDITATION XLIV.

" — give Diligence to make your Calling and Election
fure."   2 Pet. i. 10.

HAPPY are they who have fo much Employment,
that there remains no room for idle Thoughts !

(9) Pfal. xvii. 5.

Whom nothing diverts from their chief Concern,
of feeking to make their Election fure :
Who, while their Bodies are bow'd down with
Labour,
can freely raife up their Minds to Heaven.

Happieft of all, O Lord, are they
whofe very Bufinefs is thy Service !

Who not only beftow an interrupted Glance,
but conftantly fix their Eyes on Thee.

Every Object is to them an Occafion of Piety;
and every Accident an Exercife of Virtue.

Do they behold the beauteous Stars ?
They adore their Great Creator.

Do they look down on the fruitful Earth ?
They proclaim his Bounty.

Let the inconftant World reel to and fro,
they carefully proceed in an even Courfe ;

Looking for a more peaceful Dwelling,
eternal in the Heavens. (1)

When they mix in the World, 'tis to give Light to
others,
and enflame fome cold or lukewarm Heart.

— Blefs'd Providence ! who governeft all things in
Wifdom,
affigning to every one his proper Place ;

(1) 2 Cor. v. 1.

However Thou art pleafed to difpofe my Life,
in thefe, or lefs favourable Circumftances;
  Yet let thy Hand fupply my Wants,
and lead me in the Way wherein I fhould go.

———————————

Mᴇᴅɪᴛᴀᴛɪᴏɴ XLV.

" *I will rejoice in the Lord, I will joy in the God
of my Salvation!*" Habakkuk iii. 18.

I WH now rejoice in my Saviour,
that his Sufferings are ended :
  The Cup of Bitternefs is paft, never to return :
The Snare is broken, and He is delivered. (1)
  Look up, my Soul! fee thy Crucified Lord
enthron'd at the Right-Hand of his Father !
  O happy End of well-endur'd Afflictions !
O bleffed Fruits that fpring from the Crofs of Chrift !
  Hail, glorious King of Men and Angels !
Hail, Conqueror of Sin and Death ! *

(1) Pfal. cxxiv. 6.   * Note LIII.

N

My Praife fhall ftill attend thy Crofs,
and my Patience endeavour to bear my own.
I will not fear the Sting of Death,
nor the Darknefs of the Grave;
  Since Thou haft changed the Grave to a Bed of Reft,
and made Death itfelf but a Paffage into Life:
  Since Thou haft once more opened the Gates of
      Paradife,
and purchafed for thy Servants the Kingdom of Heaven.

SATURDAY EVENING.

H y m n   XIV.

MY God, to Thee myfelf I owe,
  And to thy Bounty all I have;
Behold, to Thee my Praifes flow,
And humbly thy Acceptance crave!

If I am happy in a Friend,
That very Friend 'tis Thou beftow'ft;
His Pow'r, his Will to help my End,
Is juft fo much as Thou allow'ft.

If I enjoy a free Eftate,
My only Title is from Thee;
Thou mad'ft my Lot to bear that Rate,
Which elfe an empty Blank would be.

If I have Health, that well-tun'd Ground,
Which gives the Mufic to the reft;
It is by Thee that Air is found,
My Food fecure, my Phyfic bleft.

If I have Hope one Day to view
The Glories of thy blifsful Face;
Each Drop of that refrefhing Dew
Muft fall from Heav'n, and thy free Grace.

Thus then to Thee my Praifes flow,
And humbly thy Acceptance crave;
Since 'tis to Thee myfelf I owe,
And to thy Bounty all I have.

Glory to Thee, Great God, alone!
Three Perfons in one Deity;
As it has been in Ages gone,
May now, and ftill for ever be!   Amen!

MEDITATION XLVI.

*" Use this World as not abusing it; for the Fashion
of this World passeth away."* 1 Cor. vii. 30.

THE World is still lov'd;
    and my Nature inclines to affect its Vanities:
  'Tis lov'd; and so it justly deserves,
did I understand its real Value.
  This Life indeed seems nothing,
and all things in it either troublesome or dangerous:
  Yet, O my God! are their Consequences excellent,
since they are the only Way of coming to Thee.
  This World is Man's Womb,
to bring him forth to see thy Light.
  Under thy assisting Grace,
all things will forward his Salvation.
  If I regard my End, and order all
to the Improvement of my Mind;
  Whether I eat or drink, or whatever I do,
all will advance my Interest with Thee.
  Riches themselves, and imperious Honours,
have not so perverse and fix'd a Malice;

But a prudent Ufe converts them into Piety,
and makes them fit Inftruments of ferving God.

The Pleafures, the Amufements that foothe the
Cares of Life,

(O! the Goodnefs of Almighty God!)

May be fo temper'd with a wife alloy,
that his Mercy accounts them as parts of our Duty;

While they are entertain'd for the Health of our Bodies,
or the due Refrefhment of our wearied Spirits.

Thou vouchfafeft, O God, to call that thy Glory,
which, in very truth, is nothing but our Intereft.

Thou complaineft that we difhonour thy Name,
when we only mifchief our own Souls.

—O Saviour! King of Mercy,
and great Rewarder of every little improved Grace!

Who, by all that Man can do, deriveft no Gain,
but beftoweft upon him all Thyfelf haft done!

Who dwelledft in the World to fhew him an Example
of holy Life, and patient Death!

Who makeft him free from Sin,
and free to work for his own Profit! *

Do Thou inftruct my Gratitude
to confecrate all to Thee:

Since all, by thy Bounty,
redounds to myfelf.

* Note LIV.

MEDITATION XLVII.

" *It is appointed unto Men once to die, and after this the Judgment.*" Heb. ix. 27.

THIS Life, indeed, is the way I must walk,
   but this cannot bring me to mine End:
E'er I arrive at home,
I must pass thro' the Gate of Death.
   Have I seen some Neighbour die,
and do I remember those Circumstances of Sorrow?
   I am sure the Case e'er long will be my own,
and am not sure but it may be very soon.
   Have I been visited with Sickness,
and do I remember the Thoughts I then had;
   How I resolv'd to correct my Passions,
and strive against the Vice that so easily befets me? (2)
   'Twill come to this again, and no Reprieve be found,
to stay one moment the hand of Death.
   Nor is it all, to expire and die,
and dwell for a time, *perhaps*, in a state of Separation.

(2) Heb. xii. 1.

I muſt await the Great Day of the Lord,
the Day of Reſtitution of all things :
When the Arch-angel ſhall ſound his Trumpet,
and proclaim aloud this univerſal Summons ;

— *Ariſe, ye Dead, and come to Judgment !* —

The Day of Man is paſt,
when God ſeemed to hold his Peace : (3)
'Tis now the Day of God ;
Mercy and Juſtice divide the World. *

— I conſider theſe dreadful Truths as things afar off,
but ſhall then be preſent, and concern'd in them for
ever.

I know, that *as I live I ſhall die,*
and *as I die I ſhall be judged.*

O how dreadful will it be
to find myſelf on the left-hand ! — (4)

I will therefore watch *now,* and continually pray,
ſince I know not the hour (5) when the Son of Man
will come.

O Son of God and Man ! who cameſt in Mercy to
ſave,
bring the ſame Mercy when Thou comeſt to judge me !

Meanwhile aſſiſt me with thy Heav'nly Grace,
to ſtand perpetually with my Accounts prepar'd !

(3) Pſal. l. 21.   * Note LV.
(4) St Matt. xxv. 41.   (5) St Matt. xxiv. 42.

That I may die in Peace with Thee and the world,
and arife to live with Thee and thy Saints for ever!

MEDITATION XLVIII.

" *There is Hope in thine End, faith the Lord, that thy
Children fhall come again to their own Border.*" Jer. xxxi. 17.

I Have found my End,
the only enduring Good.
I will ftudy ftill more to know thofe Joys,
and to purchafe at any rate that blefs'd Inheritance.
For tho' the loweft in the Kingdom of Heaven be
happy enough,
where every Veffel is fill'd to the Brim;
Yet to enlarge my Capacity to the leaft higher Degree,
deferves the Diligence of my whole Life:
For what can fo enrich an immortal Soul,
as ftill to be gathering a Stock for Eternity?
Shall the induftrious Bee, and unwearied Ant,
labour thro'out their little Day;
And Man, for whom all Nature works,
o'er whom God's Angels are commanded to watch; (6)

(6) Heb. i. 14.

For whom THE WORD defcended from Heav'n,
veil'd in fuffering Mortality ;
   Shall Man ftill flumber
in flothful Negligence ?
   ——I will awake, and arife from the Dead,
For Chrift will give me Light ! (7)

MEDITATION XLIX.

*The Children of this World are in their Generation
wifer than the Children of Light."*   St Luke xvi. 8.

'TIS not fo much Man's Sloth that undoes him,
    as the imprudent choice in applying his Dili-
    gence.
  See how the bufy Toilers of the World
are chain'd perpetually, like Slaves, to their Oars !
  Early they rife, and go late to Reft,
and eat the Bread of Carefulnefs — (8)
  Half thefe Pains would make them Saints,
were they undertaken for the Kingdom of Heaven.

(7) Eph. v. 14.   (8) Pfal. cxxvii. 2.

They are taught to value even this World as much
    as it deserves, .
since it is the School that breeds them up for the other.
  — Teach me, O Lord, to learn Wisdom from others'
    Folly;
to make myself Friends by the Mammon (9) of Un-
    righteousness!

Thou still performest thy part;
but how do I comply with mine!

Where's the Profit Thou may'st justly require
to answer the Care of thy Providence!

Thou hast planted me in thy Vineyard,   ·
and nourish'd me with Blessings:

Where then are the Fruits I should always be bearing,
since good Works are never out of Season! *

Of myself, alas! I am dry and barren,
and my Nature at best brings forth nothing but Leaves!

O Thou, in whom, while I remain, I live,
and, from whom divided, instantly die!

Curse not, I beseech Thee, these fruitless Branches;
lest they wither away, (1) and be cast into the Fire;

But, mercifully, graft them on Thyself,
the only true (2) Vine!

So Grapes shall grow on (3) Thorns,
and Figs be gather'd from Thistles.

---

(9) St Luke xvi. 9.   * Note LVI.
(1) St Matt. xxi. 19.   (2) St John xv. 1.   (3) St Matt. vii. 16.

ANNOTATIONS.

ANNOTATIONS to the PREFACE.

Note A.

IN the original they are entitled " Pfalms," but are here ftiled " Meditations," to prevent confufion in the References to the Book of Pfalms.

Note B.

If the Englifh Reader would clearly apprehend the meaning and ufe of verbal Rhythm, or Time in profe-compofitions, he will find them fully explained in the 2d, 3d, and 4th chapter of the 2d Part of Harris's Philological Enquiries.

Note C.

The Editor is forry to find himfelf obliged, in vindication of the following Work, to call in queftion an Authority fo generally refpectable as that of the late Dr S. Johnfon. He afferts, in his Life of Waller, not only that " poetical Devotion cannot " often pleafe," but that " contemplative Piety " *cannot be poetical;* " and adds, " the Effence of " Poetry is Invention *; fuch Invention as, by pro- " ducing fomething unexpected, furprizes and de- " lights; the Topics of Devotion are few, and, be- " ing few, can be made no more; they can receive " no Grace from novelty of Sentiment, and very " little from novelty of Expreffion." To thefe ob- jections it may be anfwered — the Book of Pfalms

---

* " *The Effence of Poetry is Invention,*"—may be fairly rendered — " Invention is that from which Poetry derives its Being, and on " which it depends for its Exiftence." But this does not altogether accord with that other Definition of Poetry in his Life of Milton — " *Poetry is the Art of uniting Pleafure with Truth, by calling Imagina-* " *tion to the help of Reafon.*" Which I think may be fairly rendered — " Reafon and Truth, forming the Ground of a Poem (in parti- " cular) or of Poetry (in general) are to call forth the Powers of " the Imagination to embellifh their Work." But here Invention is to be united with Truth, not as being the *Effence,* but the *Orna- ment* of Poetry.

never was efteemed *lefs pleafing becaufe poetical*; nor, furely, is it *lefs poetical becaufe* many of its Compofitions are *contemplative*: But, is it *lefs delightful becaufe Invention*, or Fiction, (as the Dr afterwards calls it) *has no place in it ?*

We know, we feel the contrary to all this. The Pfalms of David do not poffefs the " Grace of Novelty," but they abound in Sublimity " of Sentiment and Expreffion." Strange, that Praife and Adoration, Thankfgiving and Gratitude, fhould be lefs animating in Poetry than in Profe ! This indeed may happen; but when it does happen, ought we not rather to conclude that the Poetry is unfuitable to the Subject, than that the Subject is unfit for Poetry ? If it be faid — the infpired Writings are not included in the Argument — then the abovecited Objections, which (had they not been urged by Dr S. Johnfon, who was, both by Precept and Example, a zealous Promoter of Piety) one would fuppofe to be levelled at *all* " Attempts to animate Devotion by pious Poetry," will be found to prove only the *Difficulty*, not the *Impoffibility* of imitating with Succefs what the infpired Poets have left us as Helps to our Devotion.

Note D.

The Preface was written long before the Editor of these Meditations had seen the late Publication of Austen's Devotions ; but, as that Work is in point of Doctrine very objectionable, this Selection will be the more desirable to the *Protestant* Christian.

ANNOTATIONS.

Annotations to Sunday's Meditations.

Note I.

" *Whofe Mercy accepts fuch flender Payments,*
" *as Man's Poverty affords.*"

THIS Thought is exprefs'd in a beautiful
manner by Matt. Cafimir ;

" Parvo coronat munere fe Deus
" Plerumquè ; — fi quæ paupere dat manu
   " Dives voluntas." *Lib.* iv. *Ode* xvii.

An Heathen expreffes *only his Hopes and Prayers*
that the Gods will *not defpife* the offerings of a poor

" Adfitis Divi, nec vos è paupere menſâ
" Dona, nec è puris ſpernite Fictilibus ! "

Eleg. prim. Lib. prim. Tibulli.

Note II. to Meditation III.

The Editor of " The New Week's Preparation "
has availed himſelf of this Meditation, and *literally*
and (for that Reaſon) very *injudiciouſly* tranſcribed
many of theſe Pſalms from the unreformed Devotions.

Note III.

" *I ſhall poſſeſs Him whom my Soul has loved.*"

Nemo poterit Spem habere perfecti Amoris Di-
vini in futuro ſeculo, qui in hôc *non incipit* Deum
amare.   *Sacræ Medit. Johannis Gherardi.*

Note IV.

" *Here I repent, and ſin again;*
" *Now I revive, and now am ſlain.*"

" Scilicet illa manet plectendas ultio noxas,
" Admiſſum ſequitur culpa ſecunda ſcelus.
" O quàm ſæpe meo ſenſi hæc diſcrimina damno !
" Nec tamen eſt damni mens revocata metu.

" Nempe trahor vario ſtudia in diverſa duello,
" Ut ratis ambiguis jam pila faɛ̃a notis.
" Et trahit hinc (vitii quæ lena comeſquè) voluptas,
" Quique jubet vitium retrahit inde dolor.
" Sæpius illa tamen redit è certamine viɛ̃rix,
" Aſſiduus vitio fit licet ille ɛomes.
" Sic habet alternos Virtus Vitiumque triumphos,
" Et mens æterno vertitur orbe, labor."

Herman. Hugon. Gem. iv. Lib. i.

Note V.

" *That Day whoſe Brightneſs knows no Night.*"

In the Poems of the laſt cited Author —

" Sed neque flammantes liquido lavat æquore currus,
" Nec ſubit occiduas Sol fugitivus aquas:
" Nec premit aſtra Dies, neque Sol fugat æthere
" Stellas,
" Nec premitur laſſus, noɛ̃e fugante, Dies.
" Exulat æthereis longè Nox horrida terris,
" Et nitet æterno Lumine clara Dies :
" Clara Dies, jucunda Dies, ſeptemplice Phæbi
" Fulmineum noſtri lampada luce premens."

Vid. Suſpiria Hermanni Hugonis, Lib. iii. Suſp. xiv.

P

There is a juſt Eulogium on the above cited
Author in a little Book entitled ' *Aurifodina*,'—
written by J. Drexelius, who was cotemporary
with Hugo — on the uſefulneſs of Extracts; and
wherein is deſcribed a Method of ſo arranging
them in Common-place Books, as that they might
aſſiſt the Memory of the Student, and afford him
a never failing Supply of Knowledge and Infor-
mation.

" Hermannus Hugo, deliciæ meæ, (quid apud te
" diſſimulem ?) Scriptor miſi e millibus charus:
" Nec putem a multis ſeculis venuſtius aliquid, et
" ſuaviſſimis affectibus concitandis potentius in lu-
" cem datum. Hermannus autem maximè uſus eſt
" excerptis, nec aliter potuit. Nam elegans ille
" contextus e priſcorum Patrum teſtimoniis, hac
" unâ ratione confectus. - - - - - - - -
" - - - - modò *elegidion*, et terſum carmen,
" modò proſa oratio, modò *naturam et vitam ſpirans*
" *Imago* affectus ſuggerit dulciores [alluding to the
" emblematic Figures that are prefixed to the Ele-
" gies]. Sed hæc de Hermanno Hugone cujus *ve-*
" *nuſtiſſimas* Elegias veneror et adoro."

Quarles profited much by the Elegies of H. Hugo.

In the Preface to a late Edition of Quarles's
Emblems, Mr De Coetlogon calls them an ' original work:' But in Truth, from the ſecond

Book to the end of the fifth, they are chiefly either Tranflations or Imitations of Hugo's Poems. The following is a Paraphrafe on the Latin Poet; which is equal, if not fuperior to the original :

" There fhines no Sun by Day, no Moon by Night;
" The Palace Glory is, the Palace Light :
" There is no Time to meafure Motion by, · ·
" There Time is fwallow'd in Eternity.
" Wry-mouth'd Difdain, and corner-hunting Luft,
" And twy-fac'd Fraud, and beetle-brow'd Diftruft,
" Soul-boiling Rage, and trouble-ftate Sedition,
" And giddy Doubt, and goggle-eye'd Sufpicion,
" And lumpifh Sorrow, and degen'rous Fear,
" Are banifh'd thence, and Death's a Stranger there.
" But fimple Love, and fempiternal Joys,
" Whofe Sweetnefs never gluts, nor Fulnefs cloys."

Book v. *Emb.* xiv.

" Sollicitæ procul hinc pofuere cubilia Curæ,
  " Et Metus, et trifti luridus ore Dolor :
" Et caput atrato luctûs velatus amictu,
  " Leffus, et impexis nænia mœfta comis:
" Et Labor, et toto Gemitus profcriptus Olympo,
  " Et Lis, et rabidi jurgia rauca Fori:

P 2

" Rixæquè, Invidiæquè, cruentaquè fanguine bella,
" Monftraquè, quæ fecum plurima bella trahunt:
" Pauperies, Febrifquè, Famefquè, Sitifquè, Luefquè,
" Quæque fequi folitæ Martia caftra neces.
" Hìc claufæ Bello portæ, et fine militis armis
" Otia Cælicolæ mollia Pacis agunt.

- -
- -

" Quinetiàm Letho interdiſtum mœnibus Urbis,
" Nec quidquam in Superûm corpora juris habet:
" Lætitiæ data cura Domûs, quæ fedula fiet
" Elyfii longè et finibus arcet agri."

Herm. Hug. Lib. iii. *Sufp.* xiv.

Note VI.

" *healeth all Wounds, and giveth,*" &c.

In Vindication of the ufe of the obfolete Termi-
nation *th — eth, hath, giveth,* &c. the Editor begs
leave to refer the Reader to No. 135 of the Spectator.

Note VII.

" *are apt to win the Hearts of us thy Children.*"

In the firft Book of Herman. Hugo are thefe
beautiful Lines on the Vanity of worldly Purfuits:

" Sic, puto, dat fenibus puerilis natio rifum,
" Cùm fabricat luteas parvula turba cafas ;
" Ludicra follicitis fervet Refpublica curis,
" Hìc fænum, hic paleas convehit, ille trabes ;
" Aggerit hic gravido plumas et ftramina plauftro,
" Hujus erat teftâ quærere munus aquam.
" Et fibi cùm ftructæ gratantur mænibus urbis,
" Magnaquè fe pueri regna locaffe putant.
" Hæc videt, ac ridet, quæ tranfit grandior ætas,
" Vixquè graves fefe virquè fenexquè tenent.
" — Haud aliter, Superis dant noftra negotia rifum ;
" Regnaquè pro nidis, quæ fabricamus, habent."

And, in the Lyrics of Matt. Cafimir, on the various Bleffings which God fhowers on his froward
Children :

" Nam Tu cùm variâ fpargis opes manu,
" Lufufas lepido non fine jurgio
" Raptamus, — puerorum
" Sparfas turba velut nuces.

" Hic cùm Sceptra capit, frangit : Hic antequàm
" Geftet, fracta videt."
Lib. iv. Ode xxviii.

" The glorious things that are fpoken of Heaven
" may make even a carnal heart in love with it; the
" Metaphors and Similitudes, made ufe of in Scrip-
" ture, of crowns, and fceptres, and rivers of plea-

" fure, &c. will eafily affect a man's fancy, and
" make him wifh to be there, tho' he neither under-
" ftand nor defire thofe *fpiritual* pleafures which are
" *defcribed* and *fhadowed* forth by them : And when
" fuch a perfon comes to believe that Chrift has pur-
" chafed thofe glorious things for him, he may feel
" a kind of tendernefs and affection towards fo great
" a Benefactor, and imagine that he is mightily ena-
" moured with him, and yet, all the while, continue
" a ftranger to the holy temper and difpofition of the
" bleffed Jefus : — And what hand the natural con-
" ftitution may have in the rapturous Devotions of
" fome melancholy perfons, hath been excellently
" difcovered of late by feveral learned and judicious
" pens."————*See Scougal's ' Life of God in the Soul
of Man ; ' — an admirable little Book, which cannot be
too much praifed, or too ftrongly recommended.*

———— " to win the Hearts of us thy *Children ;* "—

The Metaphor is continued, in the next verfe, with
a beautiful repetition of the word which conftitutes
the Figure ;

" *Children,* alas how truly ! in ufeful Knowledge"—
and then completed by a fentiment which is peculiarly appofite and affecting —

" Oh ! that we were fo in Love and Duty ! "

Such Strokes of Nature as thefe fhew more true genius than whole volumes of Defcription and Declamation. The New Teftament abounds with them; and they are always expreffed in Language the moft fimple and natural: For it is not *Words*, but *Sentiments* that touch the Heart. The beginning of the 18th chap. of St Matthew — to which I refer becaufe it points to the Subject of this Note — may, in fome meafure, perhaps, illuftrate the Obfervation —

" At the fame time came the Difciples unto Jefus, " faying, ' Who is the greateft in the Kingdom of " Heaven?' And Jefus called a little *Child* unto " him, and *fet him in the midft of them*, and faid, — " Except ye be converted, and become *as* little Chil- " dren, ye fhall *not enter* into the Kingdom of Heaven. " Whofoever, therefore, fhall *humble himfelf as this* " *little Child*, the fame *is greateft* in the Kingdom of " Heaven."

Note VIII.

" — *openly fhew us that great Secret.*"

Secret is the plain Englifh of that unfortunate word *Myftery*, which is fo carped at by thofe who believe only juft fo far as they can fee. That favourite Expreffion, " Where the Myftery begins Religion ends," * feems to be fairly applied by its

* See Fofter's Sermons, Vol. I. Serm. vii.

Author, though made the Ground of Scepticifm and Infidelity by fome who have fince adopted it. True indeed it is, as the Writer above alluded to maintains, that " the fecret things belong to God," and that we are hereby cautioned againft inveftigating fuch Properties and Difpenfations of the Godhead as are out of the Reach of our limited Underftandings: But, *at our Peril* we reject *thofe fcriptural Revelations* of the Deity, refpecting his *Perfon* and his *Attributes,* which are propofed to us in this Life as a *Trial* both of our *Faith* and *Reafon*; and which we fhall more fully comprehend, and, as the Apoftle fays, no longer faintly believe, but know and fee, in the next.

Note IX.

" This the Perfection of our Nature."

The Reader is recommended to the Perufal of an excellent Number in the Spectator, where he will find fome admirable Thoughts on the " perpetual " Progrefs which the Soul makes towards the Per- " fection of its Nature, without ever-arriving at a " Period in it."————*See* No. 111.

Note X.

" For that one Act fprings frefh for ever."

" St John concluded that *we fhall be like God,* be-

" caufe *we ſhall ſee Him as He is.* And our Saviour
" himſelf paraphraſes our Celeſtial Felicity by this
" bleſſed Viſion, where he ſays — *Bleſſed are the pure*
" *in Heart, for they ſhall ſee God.*—As on the other
" ſide, the Writer to the Hebrews employs the be-
" ing denied the ſight of that Divine Object as a
" deſcription of extreme wretchedneſs, in that Text,
" where, having exhorted thoſe to whom he writes,
" to *follow Peace and Holineſs,* he adds, as the moſt
" formidable menace he could make uſe of, to de-
" ter them from ſlighting his Exhortation — *without*
" *which no man ſhall ſee the Lord.* And by this viſion
" our Saviour ſeems to deſcribe the Happineſs even
" of the Angels, where, forbidding the ſcandalizing
" of any of thoſe little ones that believe in him, he
" adds, to enforce what he had ſaid — *their Angels*
" *do always ſee the Face of my Father in Heaven."*
This excellent Writer, in another Place, on the
ſame Subject, ſays, " There our Felicity ſhall always
" be the *Same,* yet ever *New;* Wearineſs arguing
" Imperfection, either in the Object, or the Appe-
" tite, the former of which is impoſſible in God;
" and the latter ſhall ceaſe in Heaven: Where our
" Felicity ſhall be ſo great, that Variety itſelf ſhall
" not be needed as a part of it: And if Heaven do
" admit Variety, it may be ſuppoſed ſuch an one as

" ſhall conſiſt in a *further Knowledge of the Firſt*
" *Object (God) not a Forſaking of it.*"

Boyle on Seraphic Love, p. 150.

[I choſe rather to extract, than refer to the above Paſſages,
becauſe the Book in which they are to be met with, is, I believe,
little known.]

Note XI.

" *O that the Days of my Baniſhment were ended.*"

The Poet exclaims, hymning the heavenly Country to which he aſpires —

" O pulcher Patriæ vultus, et ignei
" Dulces excubiæ Poli !
" Cur me ſtelliferi luminis hoſpitem,
" Cur, heu ! cur nimiùm diù
" Cælo ſepoſitum cernitis *exulem !* "

Matt. Caſimir. Lib. i. *Ode* xix.

Note XII.

" *Then ſhall I not need its Wings.*"

The following Lines form a Contraſt to this Sentiment : —

" O mea ſi tangant aliquod ſuſpiria Numen,
" Muter ut in pennas, caſta Columba, tuas !
" Scilicet advectâ, ſeu Chaönis ales, olivâ
" Repetiit notæ tecta Noëa ratis ;

" Protinùs aligeris raperer fuper æthera velis,
" Noftra nec has iterùm viferet ala plagas."

Herm. Hugon. Lib. iii.

Note XIII.

—— " *to note and cenfure and correct thyfelf.*"

Deprehendas te oportet antequàm emendes.

Seneca.

—— cœlo defcendit ΓΝΩΘΙ ΣΕΑΥΤΟΝ
Figendum et memori tractandum pectore.

Juvenal. Satyr. xi.

Whether Solon or Thales were the original author
of this faying, " it is one of thofe three Precepts
" which Pliny affirms to have been confecrated at
" Delphos in golden Letters: It was afterwards
" greatly admired, and frequently ufed by others ;
" till, at length, it acquired the authority of a Di-
" vine Oracle, and was fuppofed to have been ori-
" ginally given by Apollo himfelf." * —— " Cujus
" Præcepti tanta vis, tanta Sententia eft, ut ea non
" Homini cuipiam fed Delphico Deo tribueretur."†

This admirable Precept, " KNOW THYSELF,"
is equivalent to thefe Injunctions of the Apoftle —

* Mafon's Self Knowledge.　† Cicero de Legibus, Lib. i.

Q 2

" Examine yourfelves; prove your own felves "*—
that is, recollect the Intents and Purpofes of your
Hearts, confider the Vices to which ye are moft in-
clined, and *enquire into the Motives* of your Actions.

But the *wifeſt* of the Heathens could not attain to
a *clear* Knowledge of themfelves; for they were ignorant of the true ſtate of human Nature. From
this Ignorance, and a partial view of his Condition,
it has happened, that Man is at one time exalted to
a God, and at another degraded to a Beaſt. But —
" Il eſt dangereux de trop faire voir à l'homme
" combien il eſt égal aux beſtes, fans luy montrer fa
" grandeur. Il eſt encore dangereux de luy faire
" trop voir fa grandeur, fans fa baſſeſſe. Il eſt en-
" core plus dangereux de luy laiſſer ignorer l'un et
" l'autre. Mais il eſt très-avantageux de luy repre-
" fenter l'un et l'autre." And the fame penetrating
Author, in his Thoughts on the Marks of the true
Religion, fays of the Morality of the Heathen Philo-
fophers—" Les Philofophes Payens fe font quelque-
" fois relevez au-deſſus du reſte des hommes par
" une maniere de vivre plus reglèe; et par des fen-
" timens qui avoient quelque conformitè avec ceux
" du Chriſtianifme. Mais ils n'ont jamais reconnu
" pour vertu ce que les Chreſtiens appellent Humi-
" litè; et ils l'auroient même crue incompatible

* 1 Cor. xi. 28.

" avec les autres dont ils faifoient profeffion. Il n'y
" a que la Religion Chreftienne qui ait fceu joindre
" enfemble des chofes qui avoient paru jufques-là fi
" oppofées, et qui ait appris aux hommes que bien
" loin que l'Humilité foit incompatible avec les au-
" tres vertus, fans elle toutes les aufres vertus ne
" font que des vices et des défauts." *   And without Humility how can a man *know himfelf?* How
will he difcover that " the Thoughts of his Heart
" are only evil continually ? "

Note XIV.

——— " *may I deny myfelf?* "

The ufe of Self-denial is recommended by an
Heathen Poet, and by one not the moft moral —

" Quanto quifque fibi plura negaverit
" A Diis plura feret."

Horat. Ode xvi. *Lib.* iii.

But what fays our Saviour — " If any man will
" come after me, let him deny himfelf, take up his
" Crofs daily, and follow me."

Here is a common Condition propofed to all that
would be Chrift's Difciples ; they are called to deny
themfelves, and take up their Crofs daily. To fhew

---

* Penfees de Pafcal, p. 120, 20.

us that this belongs to all Chriftians, the Apoftle faith " He faid unto them *all.*" St Mark has it thus — " and when he had called the people unto him, " with his Difciples, he faid unto them."

The Church of Rome refufes to give the *Cup* in the holy Sacrament to the Laity. We reckon it a very good Argument againft that Cuftom, that our Saviour, when he delivered the Cup, faid unto them — " Drink ye *all* of it."

Now if it be an Argument that *all Chriftians* are to receive the Cup, becaufe in the Inftitution of the Sacrament it is faid — " *Drink ye all of this;* " is it not as good an Argument that all Chriftians are here called to deny themfelves, and take up their Crofs daily, becaufe it is delivered in the fame manner?— " He faid unto them *all.*"

Whilft we continue in a State of Corruption, it is as neceffary that we continue in a State of Repentance, Self-denial, and Sorrow (for Sin) as it is neceffary to continue our Defires and Endeavours after Purity.

The Reader is requefted to perufe the whole of the fixth and feventh Chapters of Law's " Practical Treatife upon Chriftian Perfection," where he will find the Arguments above cited, and many others, that throw Conviction on the Mind in the ftrongeft Light.

Note XV.

" — because Thou alone deservest all my Heart."

The admirable Pafcal, alluding to the Connection which fubfifts between the Members and the Body, and the Obedience and Service that each feparately pays to the Body and the Head, which animates the whole — fays — " Leur beatitude auffi bien que " leur Devoir confiftant à confentir à la conduite de " l'ame univerfelle, à qui ils appertiennent, qui " les aime mieux qu'ils ne s'aiment eux-mêmes. " On s'aime, parce qu'on eft membre de Jefus- " Chrift. On aime Jefus-Chrift, parce qu'il eft le " chef du corps dont eft Membre. Tout eft un : " l'un eft en l'autre." *Penfees de Pafcal,*

Note XVI.

" and beholds all the ways of the Children of Adam."

The Heathens feem to have had a Belief of the Omniprefence of the Gods, and of their rewarding the Good and punifhing the Bad.

ἡγεῖσθι δὲ

Βλέπειν μὲν αὐτοὺς πρὸς τὸν εὐσεβῆ βροτῶν,
Βλέπειν δὲ πρὸς τοὺς δυσσεβεῖς· φυγὴν δέ του
Μήπω γινέσθαι φωτὸς ἀνοσίου βροτῶν.

Soph. Œdip. Colon. l. 270.

Annotations to Monday's Meditations.

Note XVII. to Med. X.

I need not apologize to the more learned Reader for the Infertion of the greater Part of the following Poem, taken from a little book before quoted, which I believe, is now feldom to be met with ——

" Littera prima rudi quondam inculcata Juventæ
  " Fertur ab antiquis, Numinis effe Timor;
" Certaquè non aliâ Sapientia difcitur arte,
  " Si qua fides verbis, Nate Davide, tuis.
" Hôc quoque noftra fuit formata puertia ludo,
  " Doctaquè fidereas mens trepidare minas.
" Semper at, heu! tantis ftupuit mens cæca tenebris,
  " Ut nequè, quod toties audiit, Alpha fciat.
" Triftibus Orbilii plectenda ignavia fceptris,
  " Poft malè tot pofitos, nîl didiciffe, dies!
" Et pueri ferulis fegnes elementa docentur,
  " Quæ levis affequitur fedulitate labor:
" Afpiciunt nigras Cadmi bis tervè puellas,
  " Afpectafquè vocant nomine quamque fuo.
" Cur ego, quod teneris Infantia combibit annis,
  " Difcere non etiam tempore poffe putem?

" Plurima funt, nullo penitùs mihi docta Magiftro,
" Cur difci nequeat, arte juvante, Timor ?
" Ah! pudet! en timeo, quæ contempfiffe decebat:
" Non timeo, juftos quæ meruere metus.
" Flagitium, minimo timeo committere tefte,
" Non timeo facinus tefte patrare Deo.

- -

- -

" Flagitiis demum incipiunt trepidare peractis,
" Ante fcelus, nullus pectora terror habet.
" Tum pavor, heu madidis mentem fudoribus angit,
" Et læfi ante oculos Numinis ira redit."

Herman. Hug. Votum iv. *Lib.* ii.

Note XVIII.

" *Every where let me feek Thee.*"

On contemplating the Deity in the Works of Nature——

" Affueta cælo lumina, in terras vocat,
" Latèque profpectum jacit ;
" Campofquè luftrat, et relucentem fuâ
" Miratur in fcenâ DEUM."

And again——

" quærit auctorem DEUM
" Formofa per veftigia."

Matt. Cafmir. Ode iii. *Lib. Epod.*

R

Pascal would have us acknowledge that there are only two sorts of men who can be called *reasonable* — to give the Reflection in his own words —

" —— ou ceux qui *servent* Dieu de tout leur
" cœur, parce qu'ils le connoiffent ; ou ceux qui le
" *cherchent* de tout leur cœur, parce qu'ils ne le con-
" noiffent pas encore."

Note XIX.

" *'tis only in Charity to make me repeat them.*"

In the emblematic Poems of Hugo ——

" Scilicet ut flenti Genetrix dedit ubera nato,
" Sed negat ut Lacrymis fæpiùs illa petat ;
" Aut qualis puero fugiens negat ofcula nutrix,
" Ofcula, quæ toties, dum fugit, ille dedit.
" Sic ego te fictos rebar mihi ducere vultus,
" Utque *magìs fequerer* fingere velle fugam."

Vid. Gem. vii. *Lib.* i.

Note XX.

" *By often renewing thofe very Defires.*"

Cicero was perfuaded that the Effufions of a pure Heart in Prayer are a Worfhip and Sacrifice moft acceptable to the Gods : So far could unaffifted

Reafon direct him; but by no means difclofe the only true Object of Prayer, or furnifh thofe Motives and Encouragements to this Duty which Chriftianity abundantly fupplies.

" Cultus Deorum *optimus,* idemquè caftiffimus, at-
" què fanctiffimus, pleniffimufquè Pietatis; fi eos
" femper purâ, integrâ, incorruptâ, et Mente, et
" *Voce* veneremur."

. *Cicero de Nat. Deorum.*

I beg leave to refer the Chriftian Reader to the 7th Chapter of the *Sacra Privata* of Mr Graile, on the ufe and neceffity of private Prayer; as a mean of working Virtues in the Mind, he fays——

" Qui Deum orat ut interna fibi bona largiatur,
" veram putà Scientiam, imprimis Sapientiam ac
" Virtutem, eo ipfo animum fuum aperit ad accipi-
" endam divinam lucem et gratiam, quæ in cor
" fuum pro Sufpiriorum profunditate, et Devotionis
" fervore, magìs minufvè influunt."

In another Part of the fame Chapter——

" Exauditionem autèm aliquando differt *(Deus*
" *fcilicet)* ut ardentiora in nobis excitet Vota, Fi-
" demquè et Conftantiam probet: fiquidem illa de-
" mum Fiduciæ noftræ ac Synceritatis, integriquè
" erga Deum amoris, eft idonea Exploratio; fi nos

" Repulfam fæpiùs paffi, adhuc Precibus perfiftere
" deprehendimus. Qui, fufpenfis Defideriis, con-
" ftanter expectant Dominum, atque in Oratione
" perfeverant, etiamfi non videant, quid orando
" profectum fit, illi apud fe vel hinc certi effe pof-
" funt, fe bonâ Fide agere, ac, poft difficilem Luc-
" tam, Palmam tandem reportaturos."

[I humbly recommend this excellent Book, *Sacra Privata*, to the attention of all thofe who devote themfelves to ferious Studies.— It is much to be wifhed that there were a new Edition of it.— This Book was firft publifhed in 1699.]

Note XXI.

" I do not fo much as hear myfelf."

Diftraction and Wanderings in Prayer, the moft devout have complained of : In the fecond Part of the Work laft quoted, one of the Prayers for Thurf-day has an excellent Section to this Purpofe.

" Fateor equidem non paucis Vitiis maculatas effe
" ipfas preces meas, in quas fi fummo rigore inqui-
" ras, nec humilem Devotionem, nec Zeli ardorem,
" neque Vota rectè compofita invenire licet. Non
" quâ par eft infinitæ tuæ Majeftatis reverentiâ Te
" invoco, nec femper mentem furfùm toMo ad pu-
" ram caftamquè Tui venerationem. Cum frigore
" meo fæpè luctandum eft, nec me mea egeftas et

" miferia fatìs acriter pungit ad feriò precandum.
" Quantâ nonnunquam Profanatione cultum tuum
" pollui, cùm quas Tibi offero precibus animum
" non attenderim, fed Te accedens, dequè Re gra-
" viffimâ, falutem meam tam intimè fpectanti, te-
" cum acturus, magni illius negotii, medio in fer-
" mone fim oblitus, atque res leviculas, quas vel
" imaginatio mea, vel Diabolus fuggefferit, fectatus
" fuerim ? Eheu ! perditus homuncio ad pedes tuos
" advolutus, ut fceleris mei pænas deprecarer, ab-
" ruptâ penitùs fupplicatione, mentem meam non
" rarò mundanis ac carnalibus cogitationibus dif-
" trahi paffus fum ; quasì fperari poffit, ut quibus
" mens mea abeft, illis Tu precibus aurem admovere
" annuerequè digneris."

Sacra Privata, Pars fecunda, p. 73.

Note XXII.

" *If my Life prepare not the Way for my Offerings.*"

The Heathens efteemed Purity in Sacrifice neceffary to render it acceptable :

" Cafta placent Superis : Purâ cum vefte venite;
" Et manibus puris fumite Fontis aquam."

Eleg. prim. Lib. fecundi Tibulli.

" Immunis aram fi tetigit manus,
" Non fumptuofa blandiùs hoftia

" Mollibit averſos Penates
" Farre pio et ſaliente micâ."

Hor. Ode xxiii. Lib. iii.

Note XXIII.

" commerce with each other."

" And looks *commercing* with the Skies."

Milton's Il Penſeroſo.

Note XXIV.

" in what channel ſoever they flow to us, they ſpring from Thee."

" Rivulus quidem Boni a Divinitate ad Creatu-
" ram traducitur, ſed Fons in Deo ſemper manet."

Sacræ Medit, Johan. Gherardi.

Note XXV.

" How dare we then attempt thy Praiſes ? "

The Reader, who may not have the Book to refer
to, will readily admit the following Quotations from
the Writings of the learned Boyle, on the Imperfection of all Praiſe, whether from Men or Angels, in
celebrating the Objects of it, God and his Attributes.

" Thoſe Expreſſions, which, any otherwiſe appli-
" ed, would be Hyperboles, do but expreſs our De-

" votion, not the Divine Object of it ; and declare
" *how much* we honour Him, rather than *what He*
" *is.*"———And a little farther he fays ——
" Nay, Heaven itfelf exempts not its Refidents
" from an Impotence which belongs to Creatures,
" not as they are imperfect ones, but as they are
" *Creatures.* —— Their Praifes may need Pardon
" even in a Place where they can fin no more ; and
" they can expect but from God's Goodnefs the
" Acceptance of thofe Praifes that are improved, as
" well as occafioned, even by their being made Par-
" takers of his Glory.——But, Pyrocles, this unavoi-
" dable Difability to fay things worthy of God,
" need not at all trouble us, fince we pay our Ho-
" mage to one, whofe Goodnefs they can as little
" equal, as they can his other Attributes. He, that
" created us, will not impute it to us, that we act
" but as Creatures : And fince He has declared that,
" where there is a willing Mind, *a man is accepted*
" *according to what he has, and not according to what*
" *he has not* — the Impotence I have been fpeaking
" of ought to bring us rather Joy than Trouble,
" fince the infinite Diftance betwixt us, without
" leffening his favorable Acceptance of our Praifes,
" *fuppofes* the boundlefs Praifes of Him, whom thofe
" Praifes (through his Goodnefs) help to give us an
" Intereft in."

Boyle's Seraphic Love, 5th Edit. p. 169.

Note XXVI.

" The overflowing Source whence we spring,
" and the immense Ocean into which we tend."

These Metaphors point to the same Thoughts in the following good old Song, which is so descriptive of human Life ;

" Water, parted from the Sea,
" May increase the River's Tide,
" To the bubbling Fount may flee,
" Or thro' fertile Vallies glide.

" Tho' in search of lost Repose
" Thro' the Land 'tis free to roam,
" Still it murmurs as it flows,
" Panting for its native Home."

Note XXVII.

" To teach us the Price of so rich a Jewel."

These Reflections, on the Distribution of Time, are peculiarly just and beautiful.— In the following Stanzas, on Time and its Flight, the Poet leaves it to the Reader to supply the Moral —

" Quod tibi largâ dedit Hora dextrâ,
" Hora furaci rapiet finiftrâ ;
" More fallentis tenerum jocofæ
    " Matris Alumnum.

" Omnibus Mundi Dominator Horis
" Aptat urgendas per inane pennas ;
" Pars adhuc Nido latet, et futuros
                    " Crefcit in annos."

Matt. Cafim. Lyric. Lib. i. *Ode* iv.

S

Annotations to Tuesday's Meditations.

Note XXVIII.

" Only my Sins are entirely my own."

A faving Doctrine; full of Humility, and confirmed by the Experience of every Christian. St James assures us, that " God cannot be tempted with " evil, neither tempteth He any man, " but that a man " is drawn away of his own luft and enticed." He tells us likewise, that " every good and perfect " Gift is from above." Hence we may conclude, that Sin is the only Property which Man derives from himself. Pafcal fays, in his Reflections on Death, p. 200, " la mort eft une *peine* du *Peché,* " impofée à l'homme pour expier fon crime; ne- " ceffaire a l'homme pour le purger du Peché; que " c'eft la feule qui peut delivrer l'ame de la concu- " pifcence des membres; *fans laquelle les Saints ne* " *vivent point en ce monde.*"

Note XXIX.

" Tho' the Fig-tree fhall not bloffom."

A Sentiment expreffive of this pious Confidence occurs in an Heathen Writer ——

" Nam veneror ; ˌseu ſtipes habet deſertus in agris,
" Seu vetus in trivio florida ſerta lapis :
" Et quodcunque mihi pomum novas educat annus,
" Libatum agricolæ ponitur ante Deo."

Eleg. prim. Tibulli. Lib. i.

Note XXX.

" *Becauſe their Obſtinacy refuſes to ſeek it.*"

" ——— is there no place
" Left for Repentance ; none for Pardon left ?
" *None left but by Submiſſion ;* and that Word
" Diſdain forbids me, and my dread of ſhame
" Among the Spir'its beneath, whom I ſeduc'd
" With other promiſes, and other vaunts
" Than to ſubmit."

Milton's Par. Loſt, Book iv.

Note XXXI.

" *I hope to riſe and ſet no more.*"

The Beauties of the 23d Meditation are ſo obvi-
ous, that they need no Comment. What a ſtriking
Contraſt this to the pathetic Complaint of the ſenſual
Catullus ! ———

" Soles occidere et redire poſſunt ;
" Nobis, cùm ſemel occidit brevis lux,
" Nox eſt perpetua, una, dormienda."

Catull. ad Leſb.

S 2

Annotations to Wednesday's Meditations.

Note XXXII.

" *Where the Worm of Conscience dieth not.*"

If an Heathen Poet, without a regard to a future Life, could thus exclaim —

> Τις ετι, ποτ᾽ ιν τυτοις ανηρ,
> Θυμω βιλη εξεται
> Ψυχας αμυνυν ;
>
> Œdip. Tyrann. Strophe ii.

What may not the impenitent Christian suffer? Ah! who shall drive away the Arrows of Conscience from *his* Mind !

In this distress he will naturally exclaim — " O " wretched man that I am, who shall deliver me " from the Body of this Death ! " While he has time, let him with Penitence and Faith look up to his Redeemer, in whom he will find a Comforter; and then he will have reason indeed to " thank God " thro' Jesus Christ our Lord." *Rom.* vii. 24, 25.

" But if the wand'rer his mistake discern,
" Judge his own ways, and sigh for a return,
" Bewilder'd once, must he bewail his loss

" For ever and for ever ? — No — the Crofs—
" There, and there only (tho' the Deift rave,
" And Atheift, if Earth bear fo bafe a Slave)
" There, and there only is the Pow'r to fave."

Cowper's Poems—Progrefs of Error.

Note XXXIII.

" *Make me fearful to do what, when done,*
" *will make me miferable to suffer.*"

God left not himfelf without witnefs in the Heathen World ——

" Pæna autem vehemens, ac multo fævior illis,
" Quas et Cæditius gravis invenit et Radamanthus,
" Nocte dieque fuum geftare in pectore teftem."

Juv. Sat. 13.

A Chriftian Poet writes thus ——

" Nulla reos animos agitat magè dira Tyrannis,
" Quàm teftem affiduè pectore ferre fuum.
" O Deus ! O confige tuo mihi corda timore !
" Ne peccem, furor hâc cufpide noster eget.
" Utilis ante fcelus Timor eft qui frena gubernet;
" Qui timet, admiffo crimine, ferò timet."

H. Hugon. Lib. ii. *V.* iv.

Note XXXIV.

" Still let me labour, still let me suffer ;
" my Troubles are short, my Joys eternal."

The great moral Doctrine of Epictetus — Aνιχε ᾐ
Aπιχε (bear and forbear) has no sufficient Motives to
enforce it : Nor have the Precepts of Socrates — tho'
confirmed by the Example of that admirable Teacher — (a rare Instance with the old Philosophers) a
stronger Influence on the Mind of that Man, who
deliberately prefers the Gratifications of Sense to
those intellectual Pleasures, which are recommended
to him, as attainable only by the Pursuit of Knowledge and the Practice of Virtue. Cold and languid
is all the Morality of the wisest Heathens ; nor could
it be otherwise, for they did not consider this Life
as a State of Probation, and were *entirely* ignorant of
the true, and actual Condition of Man : The Appre-
hension which the best of them entertained of a future State of Rewards and Punishments, was very
faint ; and even that State itself was rather *hoped*
for, than *expected*.

Xenophon makes Cyrus say to his Friends on his
Death-bed ;

Ουτοι εγωγε, ω παιδες, εδε τετο πωποτε επεισθην, ως η ψυχη,
εως μεν αν εν θνητω σωματι η, ζη. οταν δε τουτε απαλλαγη, τεθνη-
κεν. ——— Ουδε γε οπως αφρων εσαι η ψυχη, επειδαν τε αφρονος
σωματος διχα γενηται, ουδε τουτο πεπεισμαι· αλλ' οταν ακρατος
ᾐ καθαρος ο νους εκκριθη, τοτε ᾐ φρονιμωτατον εικος αυτον ειναι.
ᾐ τ. λ.

The learned Reader will refer to the Speech itself, wherein Cyrus expresseth his *Persuasion* only of the Soul's existence distinct from the Body.

Cicero, whose *Persuasion* seems sometimes to be confirmed to *Belief*, makes the elder Cato say;

" Ex vitâ ita discedo tanquàm ex Hospitio, non
" tanquàm ex domo. Commorandi enim Natura
" Diverforium nobis, non habitandi dedit.   O præ-
" clarum Diem cùm ad illud divinum animorum
" concilium cætumque proficifcar, cumquè ex hâc
" turbâ et colluvione difcedam ! Proficifcar enim ad
" Catonem meum —— "

Cicero de Senectute.

But in another Place he expresseth his Apprehen-fions and Doubts;

" Hæc vero five a meo fenfu poft mortem abfu-
" tura fint, five, ut fapientiffimi Homines putaver-
" unt, ad aliquam animi mei partem pertinebunt—"

Orat. pro Archiâ.

Were we, however, to join these with many other passages from Heathen Writers—which might, per-haps, be brought to shew that a future State had been difcovered by them—tho' taken collectively, they would by no means prove the Assertion.   " It had
" been discovered, as the Copernican Syftem was—
" it was one Guefs among many.   He alone difco-

" vers who *proves;* and no' man can prove this
" Point, but the Teacher who teſtifies by Miracles
" that his Doctrine comes from God."

Paley's Moral Philoſophy, p. 397.

All theſe Doubts, which clouded the Heathen
World, are diſpelled by the Revelation of Chriſt,
who hath not only brought Immortality to Light,
but works on the human Mind by the moſt prevail-
ing Motives; by the Hope of Pardon, to animate us
to Obedience ; and the Fear of Puniſhment, to de-
ter us from Vice. Nor are other and *endearing* Motives wanting in the Chriſtian Scheme, to encourage
ſuch as have begun well, by Repentance and Faith,
to continue ſtedfaſt in well doing, and to improve in
Grace and Wiſdom.—The Attributes of God, as re-
vealed in the old and new Teſtament—The Miſery
of Man, when conſidered as left to himſelf—The
Neceſſity of a Mediator—God's Love towards Man,
in ſending his Word—Redemption from Sin, by the
great Sacrifice of the Juſt for the Unjuſt—The Cer-
tainty of a Reſurrection, and of a future Judgment—
The Influence, and aſſiſting Grace of the Holy Spirit—And, above all, an *enlivening Confidence* in the
never ceaſing Love and Mediation of a Saviour in
Heaven. Such are the ſuperior Advantages which
the Chriſtian enjoys ——

While we are in the Light, let us believe in the Light, that we may be the Children of Light.

John xii. 36.

Note XXXV.

—— " *if we vitally believed.* "

" The repeating of a Creed at *certain times* is an
" act of Faith; but that Faith which *overcometh the*
" *world* stays neither for *times* nor *seasons*, but is a
" *living Principle* of the Soul, that is always believ-
" ing, trusting, and depending upon God."

Law's Christian Perfection, chap. xii.

" The assent which is ordinarily given to Divine
" Truths is very faint and languid, very weak and
" ineffectual, flowing only from a blind inclination
" to follow that Religion which is in Fashion, or a
" lazy indifferency and unconcernedness whether
" things be so or not. Men are unwilling to quarrel
" with the Religion of their Country; and since all
" their neighbours are Christians, they are content
" to be so too: But they are seldom at the pains to
" consider the Evidences of those Truths, or to pon-
" der the importance and tendency of them; *and*
" *thence it is that they have so little Influence on their*
" *Affections and Practice.* "

Scougal's ' Life of God in the Soul of Man.'

T

Note XXXVI.

" Inmates that quarrel among themselves."

Pascal says — " L'homme n'eſt donc qu'un ſujet
" plein d'erreurs ineffaçables *ſans la Grace*. Rien
" ne lui montre la Verité ; tout l'abuſe. Les deux
" principes de Verité, la Raiſon et les Sens, outre
" qu'ils manquent ſouvent de ſincerité, s'abuſent re-
" ciproquemènt l'un l'autre. Les Sens abuſent la
" Raiſon par de fauſſes apparences : Et cette même
" piperie qu'ils lui apportent ils la reçoivent d'elle
" a leur tour : Elle s'en revanche. Les Paſſions de
" l'ame troublent les Sens, et leur font des impreſ-
" ſions facheuſes. Ils mentent, et ſe trompent à
" l'envy." *Penſees de Paſcal.*

Note XXXVII.

" Peace with the Bad, by bearing their Injuries."

The great Doctrines of Forgiveneſs and Humility
are thus recommended by an Heathen Writer —

" Nihil enim laudabilius, nihil magno et præcla-
" ro viro dignius Placabilitate et Clementiâ.

" Fortes igitur et magnanimi ſunt habendi, non
" qui faciunt, ſed qui propulſant Injuriam.

" —— ut rectè præcipere videantur, qui monent
" —— quanto ſuperiores ſumus, tanto nos gera-
" mus ſummiſſiùs."

Cicero de Officiis, Lib. prim.

But thefe by no means equal the Sublimity of the Gofpel Precepts: A Chriftian writes —

" Si quis verò me aut meos indignè traɗat, doce
" me optimam illam ulcifcendi rationem, fcilicet, *ne*
" *fimilis fiam ejus,* qui Injuriam fecit."

Sacra Privata, Pars ii. p. 25.

This is the only *laudable* Revenge.

Note XXXVIII.

" — *the dangerous Infeɗion of ill Example.*"

" Exemplis trahimur, et trahimus retrò :
" Soli nemo fibi eft malus ;
    " Nulli vita fua eft ; dùm vaga poftero
" Turbam turba premit gradu,
    " Sunt primi exitio fæpè fequentibus."

M. Cafim. Ode x. *Lib.* iv.

Note XXXIX.

" *Advance to meet their Joys, which increafe as they*
" *draw nearer, till they unite in Death.*"

" Sinks to the Grave with unperceiv'd Decay,
" While Refignation gently flopes the Way ;
" *And, all his Profpeɗs brighɬ'ning to the laft,*
" *His Heav'n commences e'er the World be paft.*"

Goldfmith's Deferted Village.

Note XL.

" let not Pride deny the Truth."

" Sunt ifta " (fcilicet Superbia et Arrogantia)
" fanè Hominibus Eruditis folennia vitia. Superbia
" morbus eft multorum communis, præfertìm Lite-
" ratorum; licet eam pauci fentiant, aut confide-
" rent, quòd feipfos extollendo ruinam fuam fibimet
" accerfant. Utiquè ignorare videntur vel erudita
" ifta Gloriolæ mancipia, quæ vera fit Gloria, et
" quemadmodum petenda, Umbramquè Gloriæ
" avidè captantes, veram, folidam, fempiternam fu-
" giunt et averfantur."

Sac. Priv. Cap. iii.

Deifm, as well as Atheifm, originates from Pride.
We are fometimes found, even in this Noon-time of
the Gofpel, fo immerfed in the Study of Human
Learning, as to neglect thofe Treafures of Knowledge which are offered to us by WISDOM itfelf;
and which can alone exalt our Nature to the Divine.

In ' Paradife Regain'd ' — where the Spirit and
Genius of Milton, tho' much obfcur'd, are ftill vifible, — our Saviour replys to the Tempter,

" —————————— not therefore am I fhort
" Of knowing what I ought: He who receives

" Light from above, from the Fountain of Light,
" No other Doctrine needs, tho' granted true :
" But thefe are falfe, or little elfe but Dreams,
" Conjectures, Fancies built on nothing firm.
- -
- -
" —— —— Who therefore feeks in thefe
" True Wifdom, finds her not ; or, by Delufion,
" Far worfe, her falfe Refemblance, only meets
" An empty Cloud.
" Uncertain and unfettled ftill remains,
" Deep vers'd in Books, and fhallow in himfelf."

Book iv.

Pafcal, in fpeaking of that Knowledge which is
only attainable by the Chriftian Religion — *the
Knowledge of Man's actual State* — fays —— " Elle
" (Religion Chrêtienne) enfeigne donc aux hommes
" ces deux veritez, et qu'il y a un Dieu, dont ils
" font capables, et qu'il y a une corruption dans la
" nature, qui les en rend indignes. Il importe èga-
" lement aux hommes de connoiftre l'un et l'autre
" de ces points ; et il eft également dangereux à
" l'homme de connoiftre Dieu, fans connoiftre fa
" mifere ; et de connoiftre fa mifere, fans connoiftre
" le Redempteur, qui l'en peut guerir. Une feule
" de ces connoiffances fait ou *l'orgueil des Philofophes*,
" qui ont connu Dieu, et non leur mifere ; ou *le*

" *deſeſpoir des Athées,* qui connoiſſent leur miſere
" ſans Redempteur."

Penſees, Cap. ii.

Note XLI.

" *To Thee alſo be the Glory,*
" *if I have not committed the greateſt Sins.*"

This Thought is extended by Graile ;

" Qui porrò tot atrocia peccata admiſi, certé longé
" atrociora admiſiſſem, niſi Naturæ meæ corruptio-
" nem gratiâ tuâ retrahente cohibuiſſes : Adeò ùt
" Tibi debeatur, quòd non fuerim omnium perdito-
" rum poſt homines natos ſceleratiſſimus, nequiſſi-
" mus, ſpurciſſimus ; quòd animum meum, laxis ha-
" benis, in libidines quaſlibet exilire, omneſquè fla-
" gitiorum labes in ſe contrahere non permiſeris."

Sacra Privata, Pars ii.

In the Heathen World, Timoleon affords a ſingu-
lar Inſtance of this pious Humility — " Nihil enim
" unquàm nequè inſolens, nèque glorioſum ex ore
" ejus exiit : qui quidèm, cùm ſuas laudes audiret
" prædicari, nunquàm aliud dixit, quàm ſe in eâ re
" maximas Diis gratias agere atque habere, quòd,
" cùm Siciliam recreare conſtituiſſent, tùm ſe potiſ-
" ſimùm ducem eſſe voluiſſent. Nihil enim rerum

" humanarum finè Deorum Numine agi putabat.
" Itaquè fuæ domi Sacellum Αυτομ̄ατιας * conftitue-
" rat, idquè fanctiſſimè colebat." His Biographer
then tells us that his Succeſs was anfwerable to his
Piety. — " Ad hanc hominis excellentem bonitatem
" mirabiles accefferunt cafus.   Nam prælia maxima
" natali die fuo fecit omnia; quo factum eft, ut
" ejufdem natalem feftum haberet univerfa Sicilia."

Corn. Nepos in Vitâ Timol.

From the Example of this excellent Heathen the
beft Chriftian may reap Inftruction.

* Dea erat, fcilicet Fortis Fortuna.

Annotations to Thursday's Meditations.

Note XLII.

" All this was loft by one rash Aft."

The following Lines point to the Ufe we fhould
make of the Hiftory of the Fall.

" Te quoquè, cui primos ftudium damnare parentes,
  " Peccati memorem convenit effe tui.

" Cùm vitæ et mortis non felix alea jaɛta eſt,
  " Collufor proavi dilapidantis eras.

" Credite Pofteritas, Adam vos eftis et Eva,
  " Et veftræ Pomum corripuêre manus;

" Hinc nudi; Gens peliiceâ digniffima Zonâ,
  " Et Pudor, et Dolor, et Numinis ira fumus:

" Non querar acceptæ tot publica vulnera cladis,
  " Materies elegis fum fatìs apta meis.

" Ordior a cunis, hîc mecum lacryma nata eft;
  " Hîc docuit vitæ fyllaba prima queri."

                H. Hugon. Lib. iii. *Suſp.* viii.

Note XLIII.

" Our very Souls partake of the Corruption."

A notion of original, innate Corruption exifted in
the Heathen World :

" Nam *vitiis nemo finè nascitur* : optimus ille est
" Qui minimis urgetur."   *Hor. Sat. Lib.* i.

Note XLIV.

" *This mov'd thy Pity to undertake our Relief.*"

Milton, who soared with the highest Flights, has
ventured to represent God the Father addressing the
heavenly Host —

" Say, heav'nly Pow'rs, where shall we find such love?
" Which of you will be mortal to redeem
" Man's mortal crime; and just, th' unjust to save?
" Dwells in all Heav'n charity so dear?"

And, God the Son accepting the Mediation —

" Father, thy Word is past; Man shall find Grace:
" And shall Grace not find means, that finds her way,
" The speediest of thy winged Messengers,
" To visit all thy creatures, and to all
" Comes unprevented, unimplor'd, unsought?
" Happy for Man so coming! he her aid
" Can never seek, once dead in Sins, and lost;
" Atonement for himself, or Off'ring meet,
" Indebted and undone hath none to bring.
" Behold me then; me for him, life for life
" I offer; on me let thine anger fall;

U

" Account me Man ; I for his fake will leave
" Thy Bófom ; and this Glory next to Thee
" Freely put off."

Book iii.

At the clofe of the revelation of *thefe Mercies* —
which is marked with the folemn paufe of the
Angel—

" So fpake th' Archangel Michaël, then paus'd
" As at the World's great Period ;"

Adam thus expreffeth his Joy and Wonder—

" O Goodnefs infinite, Goodnefs immenfe !
" That all this Good of Evil fhall produce,
" And Evil turn to Good : More wonderful
" Than that which by Creation firft brought forth
" Light out of Darknefs ! "

Paradife Loft, *Book* xii.

Note XLV.

" *we fhould now fee Him whom we might fafely worfhip.*"

" But here the Deity lets himfelf down to our
" capacities, and is on a level with our tendereft af-
" fections ; difcovers himfelf under the near rela-
" tion of a friend, a father ; difplays fuch an affect-
" ing Scene of the moft merciful, mild condefcen-
" fion, as muft ftrike even the dulleft, warm the

" coldeſt Heart. The Lord, who knows our frame,
" fees that we are not capable of beholding him in
" his full Glory ; and therefore kindly draws a veil
" over it, and fuits his feveral Diſpenſations to the
" Subjects of them. He fends a Meſſenger in our
" own State and Circumſtances ; who, being en-
" compaſſed with our infirmities, experiencing our
" difficulties and temptations, and having a fellow-
" feeling of our troubles, might ſhew how well
" qualified he was to bear with us, and help us to
" bear them ; to have compaſſion on the ignorant,
" and thofe that were in error ; pointing out to us
" the true way, and enabling us to walk therein ;
" leading us gently by the hand, inviting and en-
" couraging us to come to God through him."

And, a little further, the fame Author obſerves —

" Men had been ſo long uſed to the notion of ap-
" pearances and meſſages from Heaven, and thefe
" been made the ground of every article of faith,
" and mode of worſhip ; that nothing but *a real one*,
" one of a fuperior kind and better circumſtanced,
" could be conceived effectual to filence every wild
" pretence of that fort ; and reduce men to a *right*
" *Faith, and a fuitable Practice :* Nothing leſs would
" be able to lead ſuch to a firm belief in one true,

U 2

" fpiritual, invifible God ; and induce them to wor-
" fhip him *in fpirit and in truth ;* and affure them
" of always finding accefs to him, through one only
" all-fufficient *Mediator."*

    See Reflections on the Life and Character of Chrift,
        by Dr Edmund Law, late Bifhop of Carlifle.

Note XLVI. to Med. XXXV.

The Pythagoreans were obliged, by an admirable
Rule, every Evening, *thrice* to run over the actions
of the Day, before they went to reft :

     Μηδ᾽ υπνον μαλακοισιν επ᾽ ομμασι προσδεξασθαι

     Πριν των ημερινων εργων τρις εκαστον επελθειν.

     Πη παρεβην ; τι μοι δεον ουκ ετελεσθη ;

     Ταυτα σι τας θειης αρετης εις ιχνια θησει.

Seneca, who appears to have been an obferver of
this Rule, fays — " Quid pulcrius hâc confuetudine
" excutiendi totum diem ? Qualis fomnus poft Re-
" cognitionem fui fequitur ? Quàm tranquillus, al-
" tus, ac liber, cùm aut laudatus eft animus, aut
" admonitus, eft Speculator fui, ceuforquè fecretus
" cognofcit de moribus fuis ? Utor hâc poteftate, et
" quotidiè apud me caufam dico : cùm fublatum è
" confpectu lumen eft, et conticuit uxor, moris jam
" mei confcia, totum diem mecum fcrutor ; facta
" ac dicta mea remetior. Nihil mihi ipfi abfcondo,

" nihil tranfeo; quarè enim quidquam ex erroribus
" meis timeam, cùm poffim dicere : Vide ne iftud
" amplius facias, nunc tibi ignofco."

Lib. iii. *de Irâ.*

Much rather fhould a *Chriftian* exercife this daily
fcrutiny.

I need not apologize for the Infertion of the following Extracts from Cafimir; whom I would add
to the number of my Reader's Acquaintance.

" Me plenus, extra quid cupiam ? meo
" In memetipfum claufus ab oftio,
  " In fe recedentis revifo
    " Scenam animi, vacuumquè luftro

" Vitæ Theatrum, follicitus mei
" Spectator; an quæ fabula prodii
  " Matura procedam, et fupremo
    " Numinis excipienda plaufu.

" Omnes recenfet Numen, et approbat,
" Vel culpat actus: Quo mea judice
  " Si fcena non lævè peracta eft,
    " Sim populo fine tefte felix."

Ode xii. *Lib.* iv.

And in another of his Odes, written in Imitation
of that of Horace, " *Beatus ille qui procul negotiis—*"

" Ergo, aut profanis hactenùs negotiis,
    Amiſſa plorat ſidera ;
" Aut, in reductâ ſede, diſperſum gregem
    " Errantis animi colligit,
" Poſtquàm beatæ lucra conſcientiæ
    " Quadrante libravit ſuo."

Lib. Epodon.

" Let the Words of my Mouth, and the Medita-
" tion of my Heart be always acceptable in thy Sight,
" O Lord ! my Strength and my Redeemer ! "

Pſal. xix. 14, 15.

Note XLVII.

" *Where, O my God, is Happineſs ?* "

I am here reminded of the Inſcription on the
Tomb of Thomas à Kempis.   He was buried, where
he had long lived, in the Monaſtery of Mount St
Agnes; (this Monaſtery is now called Bergh-Clooſter,
or Hill Cloiſter) where his Effigy, together with a
Proſpect of the Monaſtery, was engraven on a Plate
of Copper that lies over his Body.   In this Engrav-
ing a Perſon is deſcribed reſpectfully preſenting to
him a Label, on which is written a Verſe to this
Effect,

    O where is Peace ! for Thou its paths haſt trod?
to which Kempis returns another inſcribed as follows,

    In Poverty, Retirement, and with God.

See Religious Poems, entitled ' Amaranth,' p. 22.

Annotations to Friday's Meditations.

Note XLVIII.

" *And yet even this firm Refolution of Amendment,*
" *I muft firft beg of Thee.*"

A Sentiment of this fort is expreffed by Pafcal, in
a ftrain of Devotion the moft animated, and with-
al the moft humble ;

" Je n'aurois pas la hardieffe de vous adreffer mes
" cris, fi quelque autre les pouvoit exaucer. Mais,
" mon Dieu, comme la Converfion de mon cœur,
" que je vous demande, eft un ouvrage qui paffe tous
" les efforts de la Nature, je ne puis m'adreffer qu'a
" l'autheur, et au maiftre tout-puiffant de la Nature,
" et de mon cœur."

Penfees—Priere pour les maladies.

Note XLIX.

" *And fum up the Profits I have made To-day.*"

" Sed mens affiduum vifitur in diem
" Hofpes fæpè fui ; *non ebur aut novas*

" *Mercatura dapes,* ipfa fui fatìs
" Dives, fi fibi cernitur."

M. Cafim. Lib. iii. *Ode* vi.

Note L.

" *Does another's Sin breed Virtue in me?* "

" On fe corrige quelquefois mieux par la veuë
" du mal, que par l'exemple du bien; et il eft bon
" de s'accoutumer à profiter du mal, puis qu'il eft
" fi ordinaire, au lieu que le bien eft fi rare.

Penfees de Pafcal.

Note LI.

" *He that with Patience refolves to fuffer.*"

An Heathen Poet writes ――――

" Dicimus autem
" *Hos quoque felices qui ferre incommoda vitæ,*
" Nec jaĉtare jugum vita didicêre magiftra."

Juv. Sat. xiii.

Note LII.

" *What a merciful Father fhall fend to correĉt him.*"

A Chriftian, whilft he acknowledges the Hand that
imparts Afflictions, is enabled to difclofe their ufe;

" All chaftifements for private ufe are giv'n ;

" The *Revelations perfonal* of Heav'n :

" But man in mifery mifta . , his road,

" Sighs for loft joys, and never turns to God.

" Heav'n more than meets her child with forrows

    " try'd,

" Her dove brings olive, e'er the waves fubfide.

- - - - - - - - - - - - - - - - - - - -
- - - - - - - - - - - - - - - - - - - -

" In adverfe fortune, when the ftorm runs high,

" And Sicknefs graves Death's image on the eye,

" Nor wealth, nor rank, nor pow'r affuage the grief—

" Afk God to fend thee Patience or Relief.

" The infant Mofes 'fcap'd his wat'ry Grave :

" He. a half o'erwhelms the man it means to fave.

       * *Amaranth, p.* 35, 37.

---

* The name of the Author of the Poems, entitled AMARANTH,
is HARTE, the Tutor of that Son of Lord Chefterfield to whom the
LETTERS were addreffed.

        X

Annotations to Saturday's Meditations.

Note LIII.

" *Hail, Conqueror of Sin and Death!* "

" Ille, multis
" Preffus ærumnis, populos ab imo
" Eruit Orco.

" Ille non unquam pereuntis ævi
" Scripfit hæredes; et inobfequentis
" Præfidem Leti cohibet feveræ
" Lege catenæ.

" Aufus indignum tolerare letum
" Sontis Adami memor: Ille necdum
" Prævius ductor penetrârat alti
" Limina Cœli,

" Donec informi Deus è fepulcro
" Prodiit victor — Benè jam fupremo
" Affides Adam folio perennis
" Hofpes Olympi."

M. Cafimir, Lib. iv. *Ode* 24.

Note LIV.

" and free to work for his own Profit."

" God made thee perfect, not immutable;
" And good He made thee, but to perfevere
" He left it in thy pow'r; ordain'd thy will
" *By Nature free,* not over-rul'd by fate
" Inextricable, or ftrict neceffity.
- - - - - - - - - - - - - - - - - - -
- - - - - - - - - - - - - - - - - -
" Myfelf, and all th' angelic hoft that ftand
" In fight of God enthron'd, our happy ftate
" Hold, as you yours, while our obedience holds;
" On other furety none: *freely we ferve,*
" *Becaufe we freely love,* as in our will
" To love or not; in this we ftand or fall:
" And fome are fall'n, to difobedience fall'n,
" And fo from Heav'n to deepeft Hell — O fall!
" From what high ftate of blifs into what woe!"

                        Paradife Loft, Book v.

Note LV.

" 'Tis now the Day of God.
" Mercy and Juftice divide the World."

"Tempus erit, quum veftra illum commiffa notantem,
" Multantemquè reos, altâquè in nube fedentem
" Adfpicietis; et horrentes tremor oprimet artus.

" Nec jam ferre oculos flammarum ardore corufcos,

" Aut timidos acie vultus contendere contra

" Audebit quifquam fibi confcius.   Ibit in ignes

" Turba nocens; fontefquè exfolvet corpore pœnas.

- - - - - - - - - - - - - - - - - -

- - - - - - - - - - - - - - - - - -

" Tunc vos exactæ capient mala tædia vitæ

" Expertes cœli, atquè auræ fub nocte profundâ :

" Inquè caput trifidos nequidquam optabitis ignes:

" Et fruftrà erectas tolletis ad fidera palmas.

- - - - - - - - - - - - - - - - - -

- - - - - - - - - - - - - - - - - -

" Ergo vitales miferi dum carpitis auras,

" Dum compos mens ipfa fui eft, dum certa facultas,

" Dum ratio, tempufquè finunt; fimul ite frequentes:

" Ite pii, veniam factis expofcite veftris :

" Ite, animos purgate ; Orcíquè inhibete rapinas ;

" Et tandem patrio mentem convertite cœlo.

" Siç Rex ille hominum, vacui fpoliator Averni,

" Oblitus fcelerum, cognatæ ftirpis amore,

" Promiffiquè memor, mentes intrabit amicas,

" Veftraquè pofthabitis recolet præcordia templis.

" Poftque tot exhauftos vitæquè, obitûfquè labores,

" Illo, quo pluvias, quo pellit nubila, vultu

" Ablutos labe excipiet, lætufquè reponet

" Sidereos inter Proceres, fanctumquè Senatum,

" Sub pedibufquè dabit ftellantia cernere clauftra."

Sannazarius, Lam. de Morte Chrifti.

Note LVI.

" *Where then are the Fruits I should always be bearing ?*"

A Sentiment to this Effect is clofed with the following beautiful Simile ——

" Nequè cùm bene fecerim quæram plaufum,
" *fed ad aliud fimile negotium tranfeam ;* arboris inftar
" ad aquæ rivum fatæ, quæ, cùm fructum femel
" protulerit, nihil præterèa quærit, nifi ut rursùs
" * fuo tempore fructum ferat."

Sacra Priv. Pars fecunda.

* Pfal. i. 3.

LAUS DEO!

F I N I S.